The Milk of Female Kindness
An Anthology of Honest Motherhood
edited by Kasia James

First published 2013
This edition published January 2014
The copyright of the individual contributions remains
with the respective authors. Copyright © 2014
ISBN: 978-0-9923891-1-6
Cover illustration by Kasia James & Jason Isaks

Orlando: If I were a man...

Shelmerdine: You?

Orlando: I might choose not to risk my life for an uncertain cause. I might think that freedom won by death is not worth having. In fact...

Shelmerdine: You might choose not to be a real man at all. Say, if I were a woman...

Orlando: You?

Shelmerdine: I might choose not to sacrifice my life caring for my children, nor my children's children, nor to drown anonymously in the milk of female kindness, but instead, say, to go abroad. Would I then be...

Orlando: A real woman?

From the screenplay of 'Orlando', based on the novel by Virginia Woolf

*Dedicated to
the Mother and Child in us all*

Contents

Introduction	12
Change of Life	**14**
by Cheri Roman	14
Expecting	16
Distance	**18**
by Kitty Brody	18
Only Only	**22**
by Rhyannon Yates	22
Sleeping with the Morning Radio Newscast	**24**
by Angélique Jamail	24
Interview with Heather Harris	**25**
by Kasia James	25
Pornography	**31**
by Heather Sadiechild Harris	31
The Welsh Shawl	**32**
by Ceridwen Masiulanis	32
Poem for Mothers	**37**
by Angélique Jamail	37
Hiding the Knives	**39**
by Maureen Bowden	39
The frame	**48**
by Laura Evans	48
The Biscuit Tin	**49**
by Sandra Danby	49

Post Natal compression	**62**
Fresh eyes	**64**
by Kasia James	64
Raising a Mom in a Dozen Observations	**65**
by Sabrina Garie	65
Parents like Amy Chua are the reason why Asian-Americans like me are in therapy	**75**
by Betty Ming Liu	75
The bricklayer's daughter	**80**
by Laura Evans	80
Full of abundance and feeling heavy	**81**
by Jessica Kennedy	81
Mama Spider's Sacrifice	**84**
by Angélique Jamail	84
Madre, hay una sola	**90**
by Judith Logan Farias	90
Failure of Heaven	**91**
by Christa Forster	91
The Maclaren	**107**
by Marie Marshall	107
Yearning for Makeover: Jane Austen, Stacy and Clinton, and the Undaunted Nature of Writer's Block	**108**
by Angélique Jamail	108
Mother & Son	**115**
by Valerie Walawender	115
Imperial Signet	**116**
by Judith Field	116

Sprinting With a Leg Cramp — **120**
by Jennifer James — 120

Interview with Professor Alison Bartlett — **127**
by Kasia James — 127

Reasons to Breastfeed — **136**
by Alison Bartlett — 136

A Century of Advice to Australian Mothers — **138**
by Dr. Carla Pascoe — 138

Time thief — **149**
by Kasia James — 149

Telling Tatiana — **154**
by Tara Chevrestt — 154

Redefining Perfect — **164**
by Sarah Cass — 164

The Changeling — **167**
by Laura Evans — 167

I am Mother, Hear me Roar — **168**

An Open Letter to my Son — **170**
by Gemma Wright — 170

Letter to a Boy on his 21st Birthday — **172**
by Khaalidah Muhammad-Ali — 172

Reading my son — **175**
by Marie Marshall — 175

Thoughts on Being a Mother — **176**
by Mary Jeavons — 176

Something Like Survivor's Guilt — **182**
by Angélique Jamail — 182

Filialpiety 孝	**183**
by Valerie Walawender	183
Interview with Dr. Tram Nguyen	**186**
by Kasia James	186
A teenage pregnancy	**195**
by Marie Marshall	195
My Real Mother	**196**
by Judith Dickerman-Nelson	196
Tin-Can	**202**
by Sandra Danby	202
Living Backwards	**204**
by Judy McKinty	204
Contributors	**206**
Discussion Questions	**218**

Introduction

Becoming a mother is surely one of the biggest changes and challenges in a woman's life. It is at once an absolutely unique experience, and yet one which is so common that it is often dismissed. Motherhood is intense, relentless and absorbing, in all senses of the word.

In a moment, you are transformed from ultimately only having to care for one person - yourself- to needing to care for two. The new life you have brought into the world cannot survive without your help and protection. It's an enormous responsibility, and one which most women take seriously, investing their love, time, thought, money and enormous stores of patience and good humour. Being a mother will be one of the most influential relationships of your life: your actions and words will help to shape a new human being.

However, popular culture seems to have a mixed view of motherhood. On one hand, mothers are a valuable market, which can be ruthlessly exploited through a mixture of guilt, competition and misinformation. On the other, sometimes they are patronized, losing their identities and apparently their intelligence in a pink mist of 'baby brain'. In a culture in love with uninhibited youth, a woman with a child can be made to feel suddenly less attractive. People may assume that her career will be compromised, and that she can no longer be a dedicated worker.

At the same time, we have changed culturally in the West. In the past, motherhood was an expected and almost inevitable part of life for most women, with the support of extended families and smaller communities. Now, it is not unusual if the first newborn baby a woman holds is her own, and while there is a deluge of advice from 'experts', it can be hard for her to find her own path.

We recognize the crucial role that fathers and other carers can and do play in children's lives, but in this anthology, we would like to explore the experience of motherhood. Some of the issues discussed are inevitably associated solely with being a woman: like breastfeeding and giving birth. Others have more to do with the cultural expectations and limitations which still exist for women.

This book is intended to provide an honest view of motherhood, free of the hidden agendas of marketing or the medical wisdom of the day. In this collection, you will find what it is really like to have a new child; how that child might change you; and some of the challenges you will face, both when they are little and as they grow. There is no pretence that all families are perfect, or that mothers always know what they are doing. Some of the stories will touch you, and some may challenge you, but all will give a greater understanding of what motherhood has meant to 'ordinary' women around the world. Unbounded joy and delights are reflected, as are some of the tougher times. In diversity, we hope to encourage you to think and feel about motherhood in a deeper and different way. There is no 'right' way to be a mother, but whatever path you choose, you will not be alone.

Change of Life
by Cheri Roman

First day,
Halls ring with fond hellos and the growls of those who'd rather not see or be here.
Pencil dust and posters tucked neatly onto walls of pale yellow welcome the fellows who've spent
the summer at the beach, just out of reach of lessons and tensions and exams.
Midweek, midstride, the call comes just before midnight.
Come, I need you.
Hurtling through the dark towards the new spark, pushing toward the light of a new life joining us with a cry from two throats, two hearts now separate for the first time, no longer beating in tandem but still attached.
Fierce and lovely, reaching for me, don't go, stay, I need you.
Shh, I'm here, I'm not going anywhere.
Tears and the fear that I will not be enough, but none of that, swallow it back, a swift caress and
I can't do this,
Yes, you can.
And you do.
And she is beautiful.
Fall into bed, rise again,
for the crowded halls and mixed attitudes presented with smiles and frowns,
Rush forward on a new track with the same cargo travelling on cracking rails to an unknown destination, without the proper fuel or a conductor who knows how to conduct but, we have to keep moving forward and then,
it's the end of the beginning.
I go home to the best beginning one can have.
Warm smiles and full souls, lovely words with a gentle rhythm,

Shh, shh, rock, sleep, play, run, laugh, hug, haunt my heart forever.
Two squeezing into the place of one and finding more than enough room,
am I surprised? No.
The memory of what was overlaps today's newness and brings the circle closed without seam and only a little sweet/sharp pain.

Expecting

MOSTLY C. Pregnant diva. While it's lovely to be spoilt when pregnant, you're asking for too much. And you'll want to save up those favours for when the baby arrives.

Eat just the right foods

"My skin was sensitive so my regular Brazilian wax felt more painful than usual. Having it done with a massive belly is rather awkward

Have your 3D photos and this 4D video keepsake forever recorded on DVD

Don't allow your health to take a back seat – here's our guide to maintaining a happy derrière

"I CRIED when my husband came back with the WRONG BRAND of orange juice!"

During pregnancy, I recommend that women wax every three to six weeks."

Exercise the safe way

I will "finally feel con when I have a baby.

HATE FOR WATERS TO IN PUBLIC"

hopping for baby clothes is exciting; everything ju looks so tiny and cute!

OH YES, YOU CAN!
- AFFORD A BABY
- ENJOY CHILDBIRTH
- BREASTFEED

How and wher an indulgent g before bub arr

ouldn't I be eating?

My partner is desperate to be at the birth, but I'm worried he won't find me attractive afterwards.

Find the perfect maternity jeans

Even lyi cut off the baby's bloo

natural tummy oil! It's ainst stretchmarks, but els and smells so good?

SEX TOYS CAN CAUSE INFECTION

The new mum to baby bo a feminine and edgy pr

EG FASHIONISTA

Is baby a boy or a girl?

I am fourth chil problem I' I really hop

Designer Hospital Gowns

Fancy ki and orde maternit

eat too much because aby's risk of obesity and ld you diet - for the

"The chic alternative in the maternity ward"

Capture baby's arrival with on-the-go gadgets

Find out which names are the most popular among the world's kings, queens, princes and princesses. With the right name, your little girl could one day marry a handsome prince!

Look and feel gor you get active – at t studio and in the

pping list but don't know start? We've mapped out must see baby stores

The mum-to-be keeps it low-key after a pamper session at a nail salon.

Choose your labour music

We take a look inside the birthing s mega celebs to see how their labou

use you're expecting doesn't mean you can't be a style-setter

Do you find yourself stand front of a full wardrobe ir morning, with nothing to your pregnant belly in?

t how to make your beauty routine safe and totally preg-friendly

Considering the average woman absorbs up to two kilograms of cosmetics per year, it's a no-brainer to realise you should review what you put on your face during pregnancy.

"**Motor vehicle crashes** for four of five deaths t among unborn babies of women who experience

ANT WITH HER SECOND CHILD, THE AS THE SULTRY MUM-TO-BE LOOK DOWN PAT

"You forget about the pain the minute you give birth!"

How is the nurs coming along?

ake your workout wardrobe bump-friendly

Avoid too much stre

The fashionista in you may not realise that your handbag will no longer be your handbag once baby arrives. Take a little piece of luxury with you to hospital and stow it in your bedside table.

very mum-to-be comes with her own set of weird and wonderful cravings.

Tired of harassing your partner to put together the cot or paint the nursery?

Use a phone app to time your contractions

The big moment has arrived and you're off to give birth. Here's the best gear to pack

Prepare your nipples

A great way to keep your legs healthy and energised during pregnancy is to wear gradient compression hosiery.

Is it safe to eat pasteurised soft cheese? The US Centers for Disease Control says yes; the UK's Health Protection Agency says no.

Distance
by Kitty Brody

"I don't think I ever want to have children." I said this, to my boyfriend's Mother one morning over coffee. She put her cup down, and turned to her son aghast. "Did you know this?!"

"Yes."

"Well, what will you do?" He sidestepped the conversation. We were in our mid twenties and had just started living together. I'd never been able to make predictions where children were concerned. I didn't have any idea for names, whether I'd like a boy, a girl, two, three. I couldn't imagine myself like that. Perhaps I was missing a vital gene? I didn't think it was an option, that side of things wasn't me.

Almost five years later, and it's the hottest Saturday of the year, and my two toddlers are playing in the Princess Diana Memorial Fountain in Kensington Gardens. My two year old daughter has a swim nappy, which I love because it makes her look even more like a baby. My baby. She also has a bright pink polkadot Peppa Pig swimming costume, and various chocolate stains around her mouth. Her hair is yellow and white blonde and sticks up in mad peaks around her little head, above her pixie ears, styled as thus with sun cream. My son, three and a half, has some extremely funky board shorts on, no nappy, he's potty trained and A Big Boy. His mop of blonde hair falls on his beautiful golden face, but you can't help but notice his huge azure eyes framed with the longest, darkest lashes you've ever seen. Every parent thinks their children are beautiful, and I'm no exception to the rule. I am so proud of my beautiful, clever and sensitive children. Sometimes I think I must be glowing with pride, beacon-like and neon. Before we walk over to the fountain, their father calls them over from their mischief and playing, and asks my son to get his sister. He carefully takes her hand 'Come on, my sister' and leads her over to us. She dutifully lets herself be guided. The love they have for each other, the bond they have, the mere 19 months between them, is an awesome sight to behold.

My son walks around the fountain. It's not so much a fountain as a big circular stream, in a loop. The current is quite strong in places, and it's also quite deep in others. He's not scared. He's bold, but careful. Next to the fountain, I walk alongside him. "Seb, take my hand."
"No, fankoo Mama. I'm okay,"
"Are you sure?"
"Yes."
"I'm just here then, Seb."
We walk around. Twice, a third time. On our fourth time, it occurs to me. What a brilliant analogy this is. I'll always be hovering around the periphery, just on the edge. My children are going to be fine, they're great. But I'll never stop looking, never stop watching for them. I'm always here, ready to take their hand. I'm a step back, because that's where I need to be at this moment, but my love is right there, right in front of them, behind them, and all around them.

I think these few hours, this specific moment will stay with me forever, because it's the moment I stopped feeling tense, and guilty and realised that my children do know how much I love them. They feel happy, they feel safe and they feel loved. Even though I'm not there every second of the day anymore, they don't doubt the love I have for them. Not for one second. Distance and time makes things awkward between adults, a love lost. But not for children, they don't see things like that. All they know is that I'm their Mum. And I love them.

Children see the truth, and this is an absolute truth.

My daughter isn't actually two yet. She's two at the end of the month. If you ask her who's birthday it is next, she'll point to herself and say "Ah...me!". If you talk about babies, she says "That's me. I'm baby."

She looks like a baby. She hasn't that much hair yet and is all huge blue eyes and gorgeous kissable cheeks. Sometimes she'd lie next to me in bed, first thing in the morning, demanding a breastfeed, and I'd languidly and sleepily oblige. The best way to wake up in the morning, was by sniffing the top of her warm head. No better scent than that of your own baby. I'd cover her in kisses, from her perfect tiny pink toes, to the tip of her gorgeous button nose. It took me a while to bond with my son, but it was immediate with my daughter. I remember uploading photos online of her snoozing next to me, circa three weeks old, captioned with 'So in love with my baby girl'. True love.

Motherhood doesn't look the way I thought it would. This wasn't the package I was sold, this wasn't how it was meant to be, but for now this is how it has to be. I am no longer living with my husband, and my children. My husband and I are separated, and divorcing. That is a big word. Divorce. Bigger than Marriage, it's the final nail in the coffin, so serious and macabre. I suppose you could say I am an absent Mother, even though nothing could be further than the truth. I'm not with my children 24/7 anymore, because I'm no longer in the role of a full-time stay at home Mum. My children are always, constantly and harrowingly in my thoughts. My children are happy, healthy and loved so, so much. I see them as much as I can.

"But...what are you doing?". I'll tell you, shall I? I am avoiding certain shops because their baby aisles are too near the toothbrush aisles. I am avoiding tweeting at certain times because I cannot stand all the references to people's children. I am squeezing my eyes shut and pretending I'm asleep when I see babies on the tube. I'm feeling guilty. All the time. Guilty that my 23 month old daughter is teething, and I can't be there to help her, to tag team through the awful nights with her father. Guilty that I can't provide them with more financial assistance just yet. Guilty that their Dad is doing everything and must be absolutely shattered. I feel silenced. I feel liberated. And, I am feeling worried. About everything. What's going to happen? What do people think of me? Always worrying about what people think of me. I'm jealous. Jealous that their father has the confidence and enthusiasm to take them to two different playgroups a day. I was always so anxious, so scared, so exhausted. I saw the journey there as a huge obstacle in my way. A bus, sometimes two. My three year old on foot, or standing on the back of the pushchair, with his baby sister sitting in the pushchair, normally screeching "Out! I get out!"

Sometimes, though. Sometimes I don't think about my children. And that's when the guilt creeps in, just there in the background at first "Hey. Hey, what are you doing?" until it's there, right up in front of me, in my face "Why aren't you doing more? Why aren't you thinking about your children? Why aren't you calling them, why aren't you trying to see them?"

Sometimes I'll catch myself laughing about something, recounting a time from the past, before I was Mrs, before I was Mum and I'll think "Who are you kidding?". I am so, so tired of beating myself up. I am so tired of trying to explain my actions, explain myself. There are parts of me that aren't anything to do with children, that they have no bearing on, when I'm just Me, not Me The Mum. I know I'm not a monster. I'm just one person, one woman, and sometimes sad stuff happens. The stupid thing is, I'm not actually that sad. My children are thriving, happy, well adjusted. The time I get to spend with my children, no matter how brief it may be, is a thousand times better than it was before our situation changed, because we're all Going To Be Okay now.

Only Only
by Rhyannon Yates

You'll spoil her
She needs to learn
Independent
I hear the words
As I lie down with you
Your hands grab my neck
Pull me close
Play in my hair
My hair is your favourite
Your security blanket
Your face is buried in mine
And your breath on my cheek
Is hot and sticky and loud
I pull away, just a bit
You hold tight, pull me close again
Don't go, mama.
Your toddler feet kick my belly
And from inside
Baby feet kick you back.
For now, for this moment,
You are my only baby.
For a little while longer
I am your mommy, no one else's
So I memorize you in this moment
Twenty one months, four days
Long eyelashes
Baby cheeks thinning into girlhood
Sweet mouth that will always hold the baby you were
I am yours and you are mine
You are my only
I am your only
For now.
So I lie with you

Spoiling you
Spoiling me
Before we both have to share
I grasp this moment
Hold to it tight
Before your mama is another's mama too
Before my baby is someone's sister
For now, I will be yours
I will hold you tight and play in your hair
Whisper "I love you, beautiful girl,"
Not worry that I am spoiling you
My only only

Sleeping with the Morning Radio Newscast
by Angélique Jamail

She's three years old and makes
our morning bed too small.
I'm pushed to the edge, free of pillow
and under a slice of blanket, hovering
on the border of sleep, but god,
god, I'll take it. The alarm
will sound in half an hour.

> I'm dreaming we're sudden refugees.
> You grab our daughter and I'll
> fetch the baby, call the real estate agent
> to sell our house for ready cash, pack
> a lunch, get out before the troops come
> through. I hate this anxious running, hate
> that we're not in the same space. We make
> a good team outside of a crisis.
>
> We run down separate corridors, frantic
> goals in mind, dodging the ranks of aimless
> masses glutting the place.

In the back of where I'm almost awake,
I can feel this is not real. I know I must get up,
get up, shower, dress, haul the family out to
our day. On four hours of sleep, the anxious
turn of the daily wheel creaks in time with
our morning siren.

Our daughter stretches me out of bed. The baby
cries for milk. Fuzzy, I wander the hall
between crib and rocker,

and you turn the shower on.

Interview with Heather Harris
March 2013

by Kasia James

Meeting Heather Harris for the first time, it is hard not to be struck by her robust common sense. She sports dynamic hair and an elegant tattoo of an elephant on one ankle. This is a woman unafraid of telling it like it is, which is genuinely refreshing in the medical field in which she works.

A midwife of over forty years experience, and a lactation consultant for over twenty, Heather is a highly experienced professional. In 2001, feeling that she was getting towards the end of her career and having nothing to prove, she started to work with Médecins Sans Frontièrs, in such places as Ivory Coast, South Sudan and Northern Sri Lanka. It was after working intermittently for more than two years in the rebel held west of Ivory Coast that she acquired her tattoo, to represent her love of the people, and as she tells me later, "because female elephants are matriarchs, they are big, they are very intelligent and loyal, they never forget and can cry."

She has seen things which would drive most people to tears, and which many of us would rather avoid having to think about. Heather has a different take on the poverty and desperation of the countries she works in with Médecins Sans Frontièrs. "I feel very guilty living in this great big fat gorgeous country, and just because I don't want to look at it doesn't mean that it's not happening. All I can do is be there, walk with them and witness it."

Of her work with MSF, she says, "I'm never happier than when I'm knee deep in blood and gore. I love it - I love the challenge of it. You go over as an expatriate midwife, and you're normally the manager of whatever place you end up in, and that in itself is an interesting experience. You think, here am I, some foreigner coming in, who knows nothing about the place, and I'm now 'in charge' of all these remarkable people who know exactly what they're doing! It brings up a whole lot of questions about 'What are we doing here? And should we be?' But with MSF, it's usually an emergency type situation. They are usually places where there is war, or a natural disaster."

She is characteristically humble about her usefulness to the hospitals overseas. "I learn so much from them. They teach me, all the time. The staff in these different countries - my goodness me, it's just gobsmacking. I've only been in two hospitals with running water. There is nothing.

I was in Northern Sri Lanka during the terrible war there, and they had absolutely nothing. We were in the Tamil Tiger area, and the Sri Lankan government would allow nothing to come across the lines without them ticking every box. So they could say how many needles, how many syringes, how many everything. If they decided that they didn't want you to have it, well you couldn't have it."

Being brought up in the country, "dirt poor, and with no hot water," has given her a resilience to some of the privations that a younger midwife might struggle with. However, in some ways attitudes are startlingly different.

Many babies born are small, due to malnutrition, anaemia, malaria and other infections. Those under 1200g are often left to die, or sent home with their mothers, knowing that they won't make it. "*Laissez-da!* Leave it. Too small. Is finish. Don't worry," is something that she heard over and over again, because there simply are not the resources to help, and mothers may have ten other children at home. To Heather, this was an anathema to her ethics, and she worked hard to give some of these children the first helping hand they needed.

"I couldn't let them go. I cannot send home a baby full of life force, screaming it's head off, knowing that it's going to die, when with a bit of care it might make it. I can't do that. I won't do that," she says. Simply wrapping the child, keeping it warm, is a first step to survival. "We started calling them 'Little Prince, Little Princess.' Some of them started to survive, and the staff started to think, 'We might be able to help'. I'm not saying that they all survived because they didn't, but some of them did. But I had to really think outside the square."

The autonomy and resourcefulness that Heather must demonstrate overseas are ironically exactly the characteristics that dissuade her from working as a midwife in Australia, although she says of her work with nursing mothers, "I love Lactation Consulting - love it!", but also notes, "Isn't it a sad statement on our world that that has to be such a thing as a Lactation Consultant?" Why? It's all part of the direction that midwifery is taking in the West.

"Midwifes are getting more and more removed from the from the bedside - it's so high-tech these days, and it's so documented, and so computer driven. It's all wrong. But we're dinosaurs - voices in the wilderness. That time has gone. It's very sad."

She is scathing about the direction that modern birthing practice is taking in hospitals. She refers to the Israeli philosopher Martin Buber, who developed a philosophy of dialogue, centred around the difference between the 'I-Thou' and 'I-It' relationships. In the former, patients are treated as individual people; in the latter more as an anonymous collection of symptoms.

"Hospitals are there for the convenience of the doctors and nurses, not for the patients," she says, and is obviously frustrated by the litigation-shy bureaucracy which goes with that structure. "The whole western world is being dumbed down to a series of tick-boxes and lists and things. I can't stand how highly regulated it's become. I can resuscitate any baby. If it's meant to live, we'll get it there. But it may not be done to the Clinical Practice Guidelines. I might not do Step 1, then Step 2, but I know exactly what I'm doing. But, as I'm a midwife, I have to ask a doctor, who is 25, God bless them, and I have to ask them, 'Can I do such-and-such?' I'm sorry, but I find that insulting."

However, Third World hospitals, in which she is able to practice autonomously as a midwife and feel genuinely useful, do not necessarily have a more sympathetic connection with new mothers.

"It's different,' she ponders, "They're pretty tough with them. They have to be. If someone loses a baby - and I've seen that happen many times, and the mother has some tears, they say 'You would dare to cry? You would dare to question Allah, or God? God has chosen your child.' We sit there with support groups for the next ten years, but they cauterise it quicker. They have to. They don't have the luxury of crying for children. They've just got to keep going."

Heather goes on to explain, "I have never had to experience what it feels like to lose a child. It doesn't bear thinking about, and I am sure I would be using every support network available to me if I found myself in that dreadful situation. Here [and in other developed countries], we have lots of support available, and as much time as we need to come to terms with tragedy and these other mothers should be able to have the same, yet they do not because of their situation."

Likewise, often pain relief is not available to women in labour. "We're pampered here by comparison,' Heather says, "But where there is no pain relief, you don't go looking for it. We tend to shape our reality by what is available to us."

Heather's own reality has been changed not only by her experiences overseas, but by bringing up her two children by herself. Now she evidently thoroughly enjoys playing with her grandchild, but after the birth of her second child, she had severe post natal depression. "At one stage I was in what you'd now call group counselling once a week, and saw a wonderful counsellor. She was a tough woman. Tough. She'd say, 'Heather, either shit or get off the pot. What do you want to do here?' She took me apart and put me back together again. I went into it as a highly critical, negative person. It was always half empty, never half full. She taught me gratitude. But then when you go overseas, that's when you really learn gratitude. My head's pointing to the sky and my bum to the ground - how lucky am I?"

On wider subject of parenting, Heather feels that the well-meaning deluge of information and advice in the West can actually inhibit a mother's instincts, and lose sight of this kind of basic understanding.

"There's been this information explosion, and you can find information about anything, but you don't really know anything. The only thing you really know about is your baby, by living with them. You women are surrounded by experts, even a lactation consultant, and it's a sad statement on our society. You made the baby. It's made out of your flesh. We're full of experts, but the parents are really the experts."

Talking about some of the bugbears of parenting magazines, like excessive cleanliness, Heather exclaims, "Don't get me started on hygiene! Leave them to get dirty. There is a fascinating book I'm reading at the moment called 'The Epidemic of Absence' by Moises Velasquez-Manoff. He's basically saying that with the massive abuse and overuse of antibiotics, yes, our deaths from infectious diseases have gone down. Our auto-immune and allergies have gone up. We've got a complete hang up about germs. Let them crawl around in the dirt a bit, and kiss the dog. We're far too clean."

It's one of the aspects of parenting that Heather has seen change over time. "There is a lot more interference now, and monitoring of what you're doing. It's over-governed. No doubt it's all very worthy, but it's taken away parents' confidence, so that you're always worrying 'Am I doing it right?'"

"People feel that they're not doing it properly if they don't have the right stuff. The other day, I was involved with the care of a couple, and they've had a very hard time in their lives. Money is something that not around a lot. Blow me down, in he comes the other day, wheeling this pram, brand new, and terribly proud of himself. 'Look at that,' he says, 'Fantastic. That was $250!' Now these people haven't got

250c. He's gone and borrowed and begged, and possibly stolen, to buy this thing. He's doing the best for his kid that he possibly can, but kids don't need any of that stuff. Just a pair of arms, at least in the early months!" Heather doesn't feel that buying stuff will make you a good parent, but on the contrary, "It makes you a more anxious parents. It takes away the innate confidence that parents should have. What we need to do is support you while you learn this job."

"That's one of the things when you've been away from this materialistic society. I remember standing in the aisle of a supermarket, and I'd been away for twelve months in northern Sri Lanka, and I couldn't make up my mind. Because I'd been in the closed area, where there was nothing, and suddenly there were thirty different brands. I couldn't decide what soap to buy."

She agrees that advertisers are very good at convincing you that you need things. "Now, I'm as big a consumer as anyone else. There's a little Japanese shop full of all these quaint things, which I love. Nothing's over $3. I just need a tea-strainer in the shape of a shark. I just have to have it!" she laughs.

If there one feeling that you take away from a conversation with Heather Harris, it is of being deeply sensible. Pause and look around you, and you will see that there is much to be grateful for, and at heart, you do know how to care for your children, despite all the expert advice.

Pornography
by Heather Sadiechild Harris

She's a mother, she's his wife
Her small village forms her life
And her days and sweltering nights
Are filled with children.

At 30 she is weary
Feeding kids a constant worry
But she inherited this life
She knows no other.

Her thin body swells again
A fourteenth gift from heaven
And the time for birth draws near
In her village, in the forest

                    far away.

So the *matrones* coax and massage
All pray for safe deliverance
Sunrise, her prayers are answered
Twin girls, alive and perfect
Then…..

She bled
She's dead.

I worked quite a while in Cote d'Ivoire and have many stories as you can imagine. This poem is a true story of a woman who arrived by wheelbarrow at a Mobile Clinic one day in deep shock after a massive haemorrhage following a twins birth in her distant village. We took her back to Hospital Base with us but she died that night leaving 14 children orphaned. The sheer waste and monumental tragedy of such occurrences led me to often pen angry lines like I have here. The title relates to the obscene waste of lives.

The Welsh Shawl
by Ceridwen Masiulanis

I understand that new mothers these days are told that they should feel love, devotion and adoration for their baby almost as soon as it is born, with the implication that if they don't, they have failed in some way. When I gave birth nearly forty years ago, I had never heard of such a thing.

I am the eldest of eight children. My mother carried us in the Welsh cradle shawl when we were small. These shawls are forgotten now, but they were a good way to carry a baby, especially in a cold, wet climate. The shawl holds a baby close, warm and secure. Mother was given her shawl by Nanna - my Dad's mother. She had carried her children in it. I used the shawl for my daughter, and then handed it on. I think my second sister was about the last person in South Wales to use one.

The cradle shawl used to be the usual way to carry a child in 19th century Wales, and probably before that, although there is no way of knowing. They come into the category of a social custom that is so common that nobody notices it until one day, conditions change, and it disappears, also without notice. In rural areas, where people had no means of transport other than feet, the shawl was ideal and so may have been used for a very long time. Few travelers went to Wales before the 19th century to notice or comment on customs. Appreciating scenery had not yet been thought of, and the language was a barrier. Until the middle of the 19th century, people in Wales spoke Welsh, and, especially in Mid and North Wales, they still do. Bryn Terfel, the opera singer, speaks Welsh, but it's not a language that foreigners usually learn.

The shawls could be used not only for carrying small children, but for warmth and as an extra blanket as well, which is probably why Nanna still had hers when her children were all grown up. It was a large thin woolen blanket, folded across the diagonal. The baby was held to the mother's left side. One corner went round the baby, then over the left arm and shoulder, and under the other arm. The remaining corner was held by the left hand, leaving the right hand free. The older women were apparently able to tuck the final corner in somehow so the child's weight held it in place and they had both hands reasonably free, but Mother never managed that degree of skill, and I could not either. I was able to carry my daughter that way until she was three months old. After that she grew too big, and I had to explore more modern options. Mother was able to cope until we were each about nine months old.

Just as well that we got that security when we were very small, because subsequently there was no affection displayed. None of us was ever kissed or comforted no matter our distress. My mother clearly regarded all of her children as a duty. We were brought up with efficiency and care, but no more. This was, I think, mainly a generational thing, although Mother took it to extremes a bit. She was always pleased when she got pregnant, but the actual child was a duty. Perhaps she had some ideal child in mind and it never arrived.

Notions of the proper way to raise children and treat babies have changed over time. Elizabeth Grant, for example, was born in 1797, the eldest of five children to a 'then' very wealthy family. Her 'Memoirs of a Highland Lady' describe her childhood in surprising detail. Her mother did not look after or play with any of her children - she had staff for that. The care of Elizabeth and her siblings was almost entirely in the hands of unsupervised servants, who were pretty variable in competence.

There also seems to have been a general feeling that rich food was bad for children of all classes. This could lead to them being fed on nothing but gruel (a sort of thin porridge made with water), and some bread and milk. The absence of protein cannot have been good for brain development, and the clothes in costume museums are tiny - smaller even than Kylie Minogue. Victorian notions of discipline also ran along the lines of 'children should be seen not heard', and 'spare the rod and spoil the child'.

Memoirs by other people of that class and time report similar situations, although of course practices would vary somewhat between classes and households. The upper classes customarily inspected their children for only ten to fifteen minutes a day: a formal visit was made to the Drawing Room.

The middle classes could hardly live that way, even if they wanted to. Whether they would have enjoyed and played with their children in the modern manner is another matter. I don't doubt some did. However, there was no reliable contraception, and household work was hard and heavy. Until I was ten, we lived in remote houses with no facilities, plumbing, electricity or gas. Laundry is hard work when the water has to be carried, heated in a pan on the stove, and then laundered by hand with a wash board. I remember Mother doing that. Bathing is less frequent also when it's a tin bath in front of the fire, and all the water has to be carried in and heated, and then carried out again. Baths were once a week, or maybe once a fortnight. All the kids went in the same water, smallest ones first.

When I was small, almost as soon as I could walk, Mother would just put a red jersey on me and put me out of doors. The house was an old farmhouse on the Welsh mountains. I used to head off and get about a mile away - hence the red jersey as it showed up well against the hillside when it came time to find me.

Once the younger babies started to arrive, I was expected to help look after them. I still think this did me or them no harm, and probably a fair amount of good. Some responsibility is a good thing. I was also expected to make myself useful and could and did cook dinner for eight or nine people unsupervised by the time I was thirteen. Again, a useful life skill! Sadly, the younger ones did not get this training. Mother got crabby as she got older, and less tolerant.

My father had his own opinions on rearing children - well, actually he had opinions on lots of things, plus the tendency to fling himself about theatrically howling "I'm dying! I'm dying! And nobody cares!" We thought it was funny, but it used to annoy the hell out of Mother. His three dictums are, however, still worthwhile I feel:

1. A good, fresh, varied diet with lots of protein. Actually I've translated that into modern terms - what he really said was fresh food and lots and lots of meat.

2. Shoes that fit, which is good sense as you only get one pair of feet.

3. The world does not owe you a living.

My own opinions on raising children have moved on again from that of my parents' time. In the modern world I think it is important to enjoy your baby. Play games with them, like pat-a cake and peek-a-boo. You'll both love it, and baby will learn far more than from any 'educational' television program - leave those for later. As they grow, some discipline will inevitably be needed. Hardly to Victorian ideals, but if you can't control a five year old, how are you going to manage when they are fifteen and bigger than you?

Personally, I agree with my father that all children, of both genders, should be able to earn their own living when they become adults. Also, to able to manage basic domestic skills like cooking a meal, sewing on a button, washing up and so on. It just makes life and the house so much pleasanter.

You do not need lots of expensive equipment and stuff for a new baby. My welsh shawl was at least three generations old. The cot was also a hand-me-down. My parents had bought it second hand and used it for all eight babies. It was getting a bit rickety but we fixed it up for our daughter and painted it, for some reason I've long forgotten, orange! We handed it on in turn to the next child in the family. With smaller families now I understand the modern equivalent is eBay, and a good idea it sounds too. Don't be influenced by the advertising men.

Mainly just remember to enjoy your baby. In Australia at least, we are no longer condemned to a baby every year. We can choose the size of our families, and there is a lot to be said for a small family. People now have romantic ideas of big, happy families, but in my experience, the truth can be that the adults don't see any individuals, just a mass of children. They don't really distinguish one from another. Every child likes to feel a little bit special to someone.

Every mother, unconsciously or not, reacts to the way her own mother raised her. Experts from every era have added their own opinions. Although ideas about how to be a good mother change through time, the best we can do is to try to pick the ideas worth keeping, and hold on to those. In my family, one of the best was the Welsh cradle shawl.

Poem for Mothers
by Angélique Jamail

We had to put our daughter to bed
without dinner tonight. She's two
    and a half, stubborn as a toddler,

and had refused a dozen different
foods all afternoon and evening.
    Now, three hours past her bedtime,

we've had enough. Stalling, she whines
her hunger. "Milk," she begs, "water!"
    She's had three cups of water already;

I know at three a.m. she'll wake
screaming in a wet bed
    if we give her more.

Don't give in to tantrums,
they've admonished us. *Enough
    is enough.* I carry her back

to her bed. She cries, I lay
down next to her. She curls
    her small body into mine

and moans into my shoulder. I know
that in less than a minute, she'll be asleep,
    if I just stay here, my arms holding

her, until the frustration spends
itself out of her body.
    But while I wait, her whimpers sound

desperate, weak, and I remember
that over twenty million children
      in the world have been displaced

by war, natural peril, and other
hazards of human society. What
      would I do, without the comforts

of a bed, a home, a structure to hold
her sadness in? Her hunger tonight
      is brief: she'll fall asleep and then

in the morning eat much breakfast.
But those others? There
      but for the grace –

I cannot tell her enough
that I love her, though I try,
      and I blanket her head with kisses

while she snores.
All I can do is love her harder,
      love her more. All I can do is

love her more, more, more.

Hiding the Knives
(My Grandmother's story)
by Maureen Bowden

In the year 1900, we sailed from County Cork to start the new century, and a new life in Liverpool: Mam, Pa, my brother Jack, my sister Aggie, and me, Elizabeth, known as Sissy. I was ten years old.

Uncle Eamonn, Pa's brother, met us at the docks. "It's a fine house I've rented for ya, Donal, and there's a job waitin' with the Mersey Docks and Harbour Board. You start Monday. Come on, now. Let's be havin' ya home."

I was a pious little girl: always on my knees, praying to Our Lady. I wanted to be a nun when I grew up. I changed my mind when Ritchie Cartwright started courting our Aggie. I was fourteen and growing up fast. Ritchie gave me the glad eye and I liked it. "You're a pretty one, Sissy. If you were a few years older it's you I'd be courting."

"I'm getting older, Ritchie," I said.

He was waiting for me on the corner of Kinglake Street as I walked home from Benediction one Sunday afternoon. He took my hand and led me to the entry behind the houses. 'You ever been with a man, Sissy?' I should have screamed and run, but I didn't. He told me he was mine, not Aggie's, and I became a sinner.

The day he and Aggie walked down the aisle in Saint Anne's church and father Flynn made him swear to reject all others I was already expecting. I tried to hide my swelling belly but when it started to show Pa threatened me with his belt unless I told him who the man was. I sobbed and lied, "I dunno, Pa. He dragged me down the entry and made me do it. I never saw him before." He believed me but I got the belt anyway, until Jack stopped him.

"We had to beat the Devil out of her," Mam said, but she was crying.

They kept me hidden in my bedroom until it was my time, and as I retched and howled Mam delivered my daughter. She was dead. "You don't have to name her," she said. "She never breathed." She put the bloody bundle in a shoebox and took it away. I don't know where.

Downstairs, Jack was playing gramophone records, but not the Music Hall tunes his workmates sang in The Old Swan on Saturday night. He loved opera. I lay back on the pillow, listening to 'The Humming Chorus from Madam Butterfly': a lullaby for my baby. She would have a name. I called her Cecilia, after the patron saint of music.

....

Six years later Aggie still had no children and Ritchie got me pregnant again. I knew what we were doing was wrong, but God help me, I could never say no to him. This time there was no stopping Pa and the belt. I refused to name the man but Aggie knew. While I hid in my bedroom she stuck a cushion under her skirt and prepared to be a mother.

"Christen him John, after Jack," I said. She nodded as she took him away. She and Ritchie brought him up. I had no say in the matter.

....

When the First World War broke out Jack and Ritchie joined the navy. They served together on HMS Monarch in the North Sea fleet, and I waited for my brother and my man to come home.

I met Lilly Fisher while I was working in Edmondson's sweet factory. Her husband, Joe, was in the trenches on the western front. Our friendship grew and I told her about Ritchie. She didn't judge me but she said, "You'd be better off getting yourself another feller, Sissy." I shook my head. I wouldn't be unfaithful to him.

After the war ended, Jack stayed in the navy but Ritchie came home. Two years later I was pregnant for the third time.

Mam and Pa called in Father Flynn to save my soul. I sat on the stairs and listened through the parlour door as he told them what to do with me. "We have to keep her from temptation and guide her back to God," he said. "Get her certified insane. I know of an institution run by nuns. I'll speak to Mother Superior. They'll take her."

I took my coat off the hook on the lobby wall, stepped out of the front door, and closed it behind me holding the knob so that the lock didn't click. I was thirty-years-old, pregnant, penniless and homeless. I fled to Lilly's.

I was shaking and sobbing. She made me a cup of sweet tea and sat beside me on the couch while her four children ran amok. The boys, Frank and Joseph, rolled around on the floor kicking and punching each other, while the girls, Lillian and Annie screeched, pulled hair, and bashed each other's heads with an assortment of dolls without a full set of arms and legs between them. I was to learn over the following weeks that this was what served for fun and games at Lilly's.

Joe Fisher, back from the war, sat hunched in the armchair close to the fire, staring into the flames, not saying a word. "That's what happens to a man who fights for king and country," Lilly said. "Let the king fight his own bloody battles next time, is what I say."

She waited until I'd calmed down. "You expecting again?" I nodded. She sipped her tea. "They throw you out?"

"I ran away. They want to lock me up in an asylum, Lil. I don't know what to do."

"Friend of mine, Dolly Todd, got into trouble and her pa threw her out. She went into service. Got taken on as a scullery maid in one of those big houses near Sefton Park." She squeezed my hand and poured me another cup of tea. "I'll ask her if she'll speak for you if you like. They're always taking on staff. Don't pay much but you get bed and board."

"What about the baby?"

"You'd have to put it up for adoption. That's what Dolly did."

I shook my head. "I've lost two babies. I can't give this one up."

She sighed, and nodded. "You're right Sissy, you can't. Stay here till after your confinement then we'll see if Dolly can put anything your way. Pay me two bob a week and I'll look after the baby."

"But you've got your own family."

"They're at school all day. I'd rather be looking after a baby than packing toffees and I'll not be having any more of my own, the state Joe's in."

....

When I handed my baby to Lilly she said, "Don't worry, Sissy, I'll make sure he knows you're his mammy." I named him Patrick, but to the Fishers he was 'Curly,' and they loved him. Even poor Joe held out his arms and smiled at my son.

I bought an artificial gold ring from Woolworths, and called myself Mrs Elizabeth O'Rourke when I applied to be taken into service as a laundry maid at the house where Dolly worked. The family were connected with Alfred Holt's Shipping Company that ran the Blue Funnel Line. They were too grand to bother with me. The housekeeper looked me up and down. "I understand you're a widow with a child, Mrs O'Rourke."

"Yes, M'm," I said. "My sister-in-law's looking after him for me." She either believed me, or she didn't care about the sins of the lower class of domestic staff.

I lived and worked there for ten years. Every Sunday I paid Lilly two shillings and took Patrick out for the day. She would give me a bag full of stale bread to feed the ducks on Sefton Park lake. One rainy day we sheltered in St Charles' church on Aigburth Road and my son told me about life at the Fishers. "Annie screams really loud. It makes my ears hurt. Lillian prays a lot." He wiped his nose on the sleeve of his best coat. I slapped his wrist and handed him my clean handkerchief. "Frank and Joseph are the best. They're funny. They fight all the time."

"They don't hurt each other, do they?"

"Sometimes, but it's not too bad, 'cos when they kick off Ma hides all the knives."

"Why does she do that?"

He looked at me as if I was simple. "So they don't stab each other, of course."

That's what being a mother is about, I suppose: doing what needs to be done to protect our children. We hide the knives.

One Sunday Ritchie met us at the Pierhead and took us for a sail on the New Brighton ferry. Patrick scowled, threw bread to the seagulls, and wouldn't speak to him. "Patrick, this is your father," I said.

"Pa Fisher's my father," he said. I don't know what the Fishers had told him but he never stopped hating Ritchie, and I knew then that the day would come when I'd have to choose between them.

....

Jack was pensioned out of the navy in poor health and with failing eyesight. He rented a terraced three-up two-down near the top of Lodge Lane. "Come and keep house for me, Sissy," he said, "and bring your little lad home."

To Patrick, home was the rough and tumble of the Fishers. He didn't want to live with a blind old man and the woman who took him out in his best clothes every Sunday when he would rather have been larking about with his brothers and sisters. He sobbed and pleaded, and he ran away. Lilly brought him back. Her eyes were red and swollen. "You have to stay with your mammy, now, Curly," she said. "Be a good boy." She thrust him at me and was out the door while he struggled and screamed to follow her.

I'd like to say he settled down happily, but in truth I don't think he was happy again until he was sixteen and he started courting Joannie Mason.

He didn't tell me about her, but one day I answered a knock at the door to a pretty, fair-haired child, no more than fourteen. "Is this where Curly Fisher lives, please?"

"There's no one of that name here, lass," I said, but I softened as she blushed. "You must mean my son, Patrick. Would you like to come in?"

She shook her head. "Could you just tell him that Joannie's mam says he can come to tea on Saturday?" She ran off as if all the little devils in Hell were after her.

Patrick was working for the Trinidad Lake Asphalt Company, laying the black stuff on the roads. After work, he'd come home for his tea, wash and change, and be off with Joannie. Every Monday evening two of Jack's old shipmates who were staying at the Sailors' Home in Hanover Street, would take him out. Ritchie would come round while I had the house to myself.

One such Monday, about a year after I first met Joannie, Patrick came home early and he caught Ritchie and me together as man and wife. He walked out without saying a word, slamming the front door as he left. I pulled on my clothes and tried to follow him but Ritchie stopped me. "Leave him, Sissy. He understands how things are. He's not a kid anymore. He'll be back."

Ritchie was wrong. I knew he wouldn't come back. Next day I went to Lilly's. "He's not here, Sissy," she said. "He's gone to join the army."

....

Two years later the Second World War broke out. Patrick was sent abroad. He wrote to Lilly and Joannie, but not to me. I gave them letters to send him with their own, but he never replied.

In 1941 he came home, badly wounded. Annie and Lillian Fisher went with Joannie to see him in hospital before he was operated upon. They were told he might not survive. I bartered with God. 'Dear Lord, please spare my son and I'll have nothing more to do with Ritchie Cartwright.' The Lord kept his side of the bargain and I kept mine.

Patrick was discharged from hospital, and from the army, with a medal for gallantry in exchange for the rib he had removed. He went to live with the Fishers but Joannie brought him to make his peace with me. "Is the queer feller here?" he said, as he came in.

"No, son," I said. "Neither of us will be seeing him again."

"We're getting married," Joannie said. "The house next door to my mam and dad's has come up for rent and they spoke for us with the landlord, so we don't need to wait, and we want you to come to the wedding."

I looked at Patrick. He nodded. "Thank you," I said. "Thank you both."

....

Jack died the year after Patrick and Joannie were married. After the funeral Lilly said, "How will you manage without Jack's pension?"

"He left me a little money."

"And when it's all gone?"

"I'm not too old to go back into service." There was no kidding Lilly. She knew I was worried. I don't know if she spoke to Patrick and Joannie or if they worked it out, but they called to see me.

"We want you to come and live with us, Mam," Patrick said. "You can bring whatever you need with you. The parlour's yours."

I noticed that Joannie was expecting. "How far gone are you, lass?"

"Five months," she said. "That's why we want you to come. I'll need your help with the baby." I knew that with her Mam and Dad next door, with one of her brothers and three sisters still at home, she would have enough help, but she was saving my pride.

"Of course I'll come," I said.

The day my son and daughter-in-law took me home was the happiest of my life.

In her sixth month Joannie was taken ill with a kidney infection. It brought on premature labour and she gave birth to twin boys. One lived only a few hours. The other died the following day. "It's better that God took them, lass," I said. "They would have been afflicted. Look at Emily across the road, with her little spastic girl. They would have been worse than her, and two of them. What kind of life would it have been for you all?"

"I know, Mam, but it's hard to lose a child and I feel like it's my fault."

For the first time in thirty-eight years I spoke of Cecilia. "I never even held her. The only thing I could give her was her name."

"I'm sorry. I didn't know. How did you get over it?"

"Sometimes common sense is more help than weeping and wailing. I put it behind me, and that's what you have to do." She did. She never spoke of the twins again.

It was five years before she next fell pregnant. I held her hands through the spasms. She closed her eyes.

The midwife said, "She's praying for a son." I knew she didn't care. She'd done this before: two babies born, two babies dead. She just wanted it to stop. When it did it was me that placed her daughter in her arms.

"We'll call her Joan, after you," Patrick said.

"No," she said. "I want to call her Cecilia."

....

They had two more healthy daughters: Joan and Catherine, but no son. I hope Patrick wasn't disappointed. I know Joannie wasn't.

The years speed up as we grow old, but in those last contented days I had time to think back. I lost my God and my son but, thanks be, they found me. I could have lived better, no doubt. I tried to control what happened to me but I had to fight and life hit back hard. The world's changing.

My granddaughters will have choices I was denied. May they choose well.

The day came for their lives to go on without me. Before I closed my eyes for the last time I said to Joannie, "Keep them safe. Hide the knives, lass. Hide the knives."

The frame
by Laura Evans

There was a tiny window high up in the side of the mountain. Bethany used it to watch the world.

There were bars on the window. Bethany's mother said they were to keep the world out. Bethany had no father to refute or repeat this. He was in the world, although Bethany had never spotted him through her telescope.

Bethany's father had grey hair and a limp and a small quiet dog. Bethany longed to see him. "One day you will, my love, my duck," said Bethany's mother, whenever she asked. But her mother would never say when – only "soon".

The Biscuit Tin
by Sandra Danby

Lorna knew she was dying. The doctor hadn't said she was, but that's how she interpreted his screwed-up lips. Her neighbour hadn't said she was, but Lorna could see the pity in her eyes. None of them were able to say it out loud. She wasn't sure if this was reassuring, in so much as IT, ie death, may be quite a way away yet; or frightening, in that IT was so close no-one wanted to upset her. Justine was not a part of this conspiracy, she knew nothing about her mother's impending death because Lorna had not told her she was ill.

She rested her head against the back of the chair, turning her cheek sideways to brush it gently over the fabric. It was a comforting habit. The weave was worn by decades of Lorna doing just this, so worn the colour was gone, the threads broken and that was how Lorna felt: worn and faded.

This kitchen had seen so much history, so much laughter, so many ordinary days and just a few special ones. Her mind wandered, her eyelids drooped as she let herself remember her independent oh so willful daughter at a time when she had needed her mother, here, in this kitchen. Not thousands of miles away.

....

Lorna had stuffed the chicken sitting in its pan ready for the oven, its breast decorously covered by strips of streaky bacon. Another pan was full of sausage and bacon rolls. On the hob, a small pan bubbled slowly with sliced apples to be made into apple sauce to be served with the joint of roast pork and crackling on Boxing Day. Lorna checked her list. Next she would peel the potatoes or, she checked her watch, or do the biscuits. There was half an hour before the Crackerjack Christmas Special started which Justine wanted to watch.

Quietly she peeped around the front room door. Yes, Justine was still where Lorna had left her after lunch, sitting at the dining table, surrounded by a halo of crayons. Really the child was always colouring-in or drawing, it was the same every tea-time after school since she had started in Mrs Plumrose's class September just gone. Every tea-time except Friday. Friday was 'Crackerjack' day which could not be missed. Justine would watch 'Blue Peter' too, but only if there was a craft project to do. A corner of the garden shed was filled with cardboard toilet roll inners, empty Weetabix boxes, silver milk bottle tops.

"Justine, will you come in here and help me please?"

The small dark head didn't move from where it hovered over a picture which Lorna could only partly see but what looked like the back end of a horse.

"It's a job you like, sorting out the biscuits."

The little head rose and Lorna was bathed in the warm excitement of her daughter's smile. It was at moments like this that she felt connected to her strangely self-contained five-year old daughter.

"Really? Are there chocolate fingers? And teacakes?"

"You'll have to come and look, won't you?"

Mother and daughter spent a happy hour together at the kitchen table. In truth, Lorna let Justine do the work for she was tired after a busy week finishing and fitting special Christmas dresses for six of her regular clients. So now she sat, her hands clasped around a cup of tea, watching Justine fill the biscuit tins. But even this simple task, Justine did not complete in what Lorna thought of as the usual way, in other words how her own mother taught her when she was Justine's age.

There were three biscuit tins which were used every Christmas for biscuits and for the rest of the year to store home-made cakes. They were stacked on the high shelves in the pantry, high so that Justine could not, yet, reach them. The Coronation biscuit tin was filled only with shortbread. Chocolate biscuits, some wrapped in fancy silver paper, went into the round lilac Quality Street tin. Penguins, Club and other wrapped biscuits were stored in a battered oblong tin with a picture of the Queen Mary ocean liner on the lid. The tin was sent to Lorna by her eldest brother Geoffrey who ran away to sea when he was 14. He worked as a steward on the ship's maiden voyage to New York in 1936, but was killed during in Libya the Second World War. Lorna still missed him, and took a quiet moment to think of him every Christmas when his old tin came out of the cupboard.

Lorna learned the tradition of filling the biscuit tins at Christmas from her own mother. She learned to appreciate it as a contemplative task. Now she watched as Justine sorted the packets of biscuits into three piles, sorted by type for each tin, then each individual pile was organized by shape of biscuit. Justine sorted with a crinkle of concentration between her eyebrows which made her look older than her five years. One day Justine will teach her own son or daughter to sort biscuits at Christmas, Lorna thought. The thought of this family tradition being passed on made her feel quite emotional all of a sudden, and she shook her head slightly to shake off the mood. No time for getting sentimental now, when there were jobs to be done.

"Can I keep the biscuit boxes Mum?" Beside Justine was a neat pile of empty cardboard biscuit boxes.

"Oh Justine, you've already got a big pile of boxes in the shed that you haven't used yet. We don't need any more."

"Please Mum. These are different shapes and sizes, and look," she held up a chocolate fingers box, "this one's slim and long. I could paint this and decorate it for Dad, he could keep something in it. His pens, or his fishing flies, or something."

Lorna looked into the earnest face of her daughter and smiled. Justine was a bit of a throw-back, some days she reminded Lorna of her own mother. She would have survived well in the war where everything was saved and re-used and reinvented.

"Alright dear, that's a nice idea to make something for Dad."

"Really? Oh thank you Mum." Justine put the slim box aside, on the dresser next to her father's old radio.

The three biscuit tins were filled, the various shapes slotted into place by Justine like a Roman mosaic, the finished result as if the biscuit tins had been sold with their contents and not bought separately in an effort to save a couple of bob. All spare cash had been spent on Justine's surprise present, hence the chicken instead of turkey this year. In Mr Heddon's garden shed next door was a bicycle, not a new one, but a good condition second-hand one, newly painted bright blue. Justine was only expecting a dressing gown from Father Christmas, who knew that her old one hung half-mast around her skinny ankles.

"Now shall we have a piece of shortbread each to celebrate during a good job?"

"Can I have a fan?" Justine carefully split the circle of shortbread fans first in half, and then into individual pieces, broken neatly along the lines scored by the baker. Lorna chose a shortbread finger.

They sat in silence for a moment, crunching, chicken and crayoning and 'Crackerjack' all forgotten. Then Lorna put the lid on the Coronation tin and gently stroked the picture on the top. She'd been in hospital on the day Princess Elizabeth became Queen, and so young too. Lorna was recovering from the stillbirth of her first baby, a son, of whom Justine knew nothing. Lorna had been adamant when she went home that life should go on as if nothing had happened, and she never mentioned the lost baby aloud again. People quite obviously talked a little louder in her hearing about everything but babies, and conversations were stopped short when she entered a room at WI Young Wives. Only her friend Betty seemed to understand Lorna's feeling of loss and her need for privacy. It was Betty who gave her the biscuit tin, and it was Betty who died of breast cancer a year later. And so disappeared the one person who Lorna could talk to about her grief, her grief and shame that she had done something to kill the child in her womb. Drunk something, danced at a party, drunk a gin and tonic. Lorna knew that wasn't logical and she was normally a very logical person, she called a spade and spade after all, but logic didn't help her forget her lost baby. So she didn't talk of it ever again.

Only once a year did she allow herself to remember her baby, and Betty, by bringing out the Coronation tin at Christmas and filling it with biscuits.

She had felt guilty then, not telling Justine, encouraging Justine to fill the tin with biscuits on Christmas Eve. Somehow the biscuit thing had ended up feeling like a double-betrayal, betrayal of the memory of her baby, and betrayal of her living daughter.

....

Lorna opened her eyes and shifted the cushion behind her back. Her head ached with thinking, the memories were difficult but also thinking was increasingly hard to do. It was impossible to have opinions. She could manage the tea or coffee sort of question. But yesterday a market research lady with a clipboard and heavy black shoes had knocked on the door to ask her questions about 'Women and feminism today: the effect on planning for your needs' by East Yorkshire County Council. Lorna had made Cindy a cup of tea and given her a biscuit, and they'd had a nice chat about the roses in the front garden. In particular the rather grand crimson rose beside the front door which flowered all summer but which now was at its ugliest, all bare branches and thorns.

"Falstaff, it's called," offering the biscuit tin to Cindy again, "like in Shakespeare. It's the prettiest deep red, the colour of blood if you prick your finger on a thorn."

Cindy reminded Lorna of Justine, about the same age but rather thicker ankles, thick ankles thankfully didn't run in Lorna's family and Justine's ankles were beautifully slim. It was thinking about Justine that brought on the tears. Lorna seemed to be crying all the time these days and she'd never been a crier; not when John died, not when Pete her husband died, not when Justine went off to Malaga and returned a strange pale woman who you could see believed she didn't need her mother but who patently needed a hug.

She had never felt that Justine needed her, not beyond the maternal treating bumps and scrapes of which there were many, buying her first bra, broderie anglais and white, and explaining as her mother had to her about what happened 'down there'. This needing was a two-way thing. Lorna knew she had an emotional need for Justine to need her, unfortunately this hadn't dawned on her daughter who was turning into a self-contained little girl, wrapped-up in herself, happy to be alone, her brow furrowed over some colouring or origami or a model she was making.

No-one was more surprised than Lorna when Justine made it as an artist. Art college in London. She was making good money now though Lorna hadn't worked out who bought Justine's art. She had learned to call the pieces Justine made 'art', rather than 'pictures,' and she even had an early charcoal drawing of an owl framed and hanging in the hallway. Last time they'd talked, Justine was working on something green. To Lorna, green meant a nice neat lawn, a sharp apple, her favourite round-necked cardigan. She didn't think it meant the same things to Justine, had thought to ask, but couldn't remember Justine's answer. And now she was too tired.

Lorna ignored Dr Hebden's advice and kept her secret. Apart from being a bit fatter in the face and midriff because of the drugs, she didn't look ill. Justine was always so busy, going here and there on airplanes to museums all over the world, but without fail she always rung her mother at 7pm Yorkshire time every Sunday evening. The only time this hadn't happened was when Justine was studying in Malaga. Lorna, who had never been abroad, enjoyed listening to Justine talk about where she was and what she was doing. Soldiers in Athens wearing white uniforms and red bouncing bobbles on their boots. Oranges growing on trees at the roadside in Spain that you could reach up and pick. Imagine, a fresh orange with a stalk and leaf. The miniature hand cream and toothbrush and toothpaste in the free toiletry bag she was given on the airplane, even a silky eye mask and socks to keep her feet warm. Pizzas in Naples which were too big for the plate they were served on, so they flopped over the side like a fringe.

Justine created pictures so Lorna could see clearly everything; she described things in such detail, the colours, the shapes, the smells. When she rang last Sunday night she'd told Lorna all about the snow that had fallen overnight in Tokyo and which had caused chaos for a few hours. How the Japanese were not used to it and tried to walk through the snowdrifts wearing sandals, how the snow had deadened all sound in the city.

....

Lorna lay tucked tightly in her bed as she hadn't been tucked in since her own mother had carefully arranged her sheet and orange candlewick bedspread so the spiders couldn't climb into bed with her. Now she would never see Justine again, or Justine's children if she ever had babies. Dr Hebden himself had called Japan and now Justine was on her way and Lorna lay, waiting, trapped with nothing to do but think of what she hadn't told her daughter.

You need to know about John. He was your brother and he was stillborn, three years before you came along. I want you to understand that losing John took something out of me and made me a poor mother for you and I wish I had done better by you. I let his death spoil my life, and spoil your father's. Poor Pete tried to help me, but I let my loss stop me doing things. You mustn't let that happen to you Justine, no matter what happens in your life. So when the bad time comes for you, and it will because everyone has at least one, you must remember who you are and where you came from. You must pick yourself up, be strong and do what you want to do. I missed out, I should have played the piano professionally. I was good enough. I was, but first there was no money and then there was the war and no money. And then I met Pete and lost John and you arrived and… in all of that I allowed my fingers to stop aching to play the piano. And then too much time had passed by and I was frightened to try again. Don't let that happen to you. If something happens to interrupt your art, don't ever forget that you are an artist.

A gentle hand on her arm now, a nurse in blue leant over her from where she sat in the old armchair beside Lorna's bed, the bed she and Pete had shared for so many years. The nurse smiled, it was a calm plump smile and suddenly Lorna wanted to kiss her rosy cheek. She struggled to sit up but the warm pressure of the nurse's hand on her shoulder held her on the bed.

"Sssh now dear, it's time to go to sleep now."

"But... Justine... I must tell her..."

"I'll tell her, if she comes while you are sleeping."

"...say I am so proud to be her mother."

Lorna closed her eyes and the nurse sat beside her, holding her hand, until she fell into her last sleep.

....

The three women were standing in a row, hands on hips, lips pursed. Every now and then, a head would tilt forward a touch, a neck stretched as if to focus closer, then the norm was resumed. The mirroring was unconscious. It was not an exercise in theatrical art, but the process of final approval of the layout of Justine's exhibition at the Barker Mews Gallery.

Justine was the silent one in the middle, her position signifying her importance in this triptych, her hands spattered white with gloss paint from last night's headache brought on by grief. Grief that seemed to be deepening, last night it had dawned on her that she was the oldest in her family now, her parents' generation had gone, her mother had gone. She was alone. She had sat alone in her studio, the migraine tearing at the tissues in her brain, pinned down by the weight of Japanese jetlag she could not shake, and wept for her mother.

She shook her head, now was not the time to indulge. On Justine's right, her agent Maud was nodding to an internal monologue, occasionally writing a note in a tiny turquoise leather notebook with a slim black pen. The only one talking was Zuzannah, the gallery's curator. She was justifying her decision to arrange the pieces out of number order, the number order in which Justine had painted them. Each woman was holding a copy of the 30 page colour catalogue.

Justine tried to focus on whether positioning 'Green 7' before 'Green 5' would really pose a problem for the appreciation of the collection. She didn't particularly like 'Green 7'. It was one of the later pieces which had taken a long time to resolve. 'Green 5', however she was proud of. She longed for sleep.

"No, you're right." Both women turned towards her. "5 has to go in its rightful place."

She was relieved and surprised with the ease at which they accepted her pronouncement. Last night's migraine would have floored an ox. The sheer physicality of the work was back-breaking, moving this here then there, crossing fingers and hoping there would be no breakages, gradually transforming the gallery from an empty room full of wooden crates into an elegant exhibition space full of creativity. Without fail she found the roller-coaster process painful, exhausting and exhilarating. Without fail halfway through she wanted to run away. But there never was a possibility of escape, never a possibility of fulfilling her desire to flee. And then the next day, she would be exhilarated again.

And now only 'Green 10' remained to finally be put into position. Justine was beginning to hate 'Green 10': because it had been so difficult to finish, because her gut instinct told her it was one piece too far, because she was afraid it didn't fit. Then she glanced around the exhibit and had to admit, reluctantly, that Zuzannah had been right. There would be a gaping hole over there in that awkwardly-shaped corner without 'Green 10'. Justine's heart was in her mouth. Her mouth was dry and she was in need of a cup of tea to take two more painkillers.

She turned to look for Zuzannah's assistant to ask for tea, and as she turned her eyes swept across the display as if seeing it for the first time. She made a small private intake of breath. Yes, her pieces did look good. The roller-coaster again. Zuzannah had done well. Perhaps her fears of last night were unfounded. The dark of the night and pain could do that, skew the facts, inflate the fears, indulge paranoia. If Maud was correct, and Maud's forecasts did tend to be on the cautious side, there were purchasers lined up already for 'Green 1', '2' and '3'. In Justine's experience, the first three pieces in any new collection were the ones that flowed, that needed no 'forcing'. Ten was her absolute limit for a series, that's why this gallery was so suited to her output. Any more and Maud would have to find a bigger location.

The room was quiet except for the gentle rumble of rain drumming on the glass roof above their heads, the glass roof designed to let natural light flow in to illuminate the gallery but which at the moment was lighting up the grey February sky outside with electricity. After this meeting the gallery would be cleaned ready for the briefing of the sales team and hostesses tomorrow, everything had to be perfect for Thursday. Justine looked up at the ceiling. The clouds were heavy with rain, no doubt the same sky was raining now in Yorkshire, over Seaview Cottage, even though her mother had left and would never be rained on again.

At last, almost everything was decided. Justine had vetoed Zuzannah's suggestion of green accent lighting while Maud had put a stop to Zuzannah's green-themed food and drink proposal which featured a lot of lettuce and absinthe. They had however both approved of one green accent in the gallery space: a waist-high bowl made from a single piece of polished burr maple, piled high with shiny green Granny Smiths. The bowl, on loan from the Victoria & Albert

Museum, was by Mark Lindquist. Justine loved it, and had specifically requested it. She was pleased now, with its effect.

The three women began to discuss the relative merits of no backing sound, a wind-effects CD or Michael Nyman, when two things happening at once broke the church-like hush. An invisible door, artfully disguised as a panel in the plain white wall, opened to admit Zuzannah's assistant. She was carrying a tea tray. Earl Grey, shortbread biscuits. Always the same. Justine liked that. Before they had settled on Barker Mews three years ago, she Maud and Darya had visited another much-lauded gallery with a Mayfair postcode. The curator had mentioned five times that she had worked at the Tate and longed to move to MoMA then served stewed lapsang souchong with rice milk, the biscuits were jammie dodgers. The whole experience was surreal.

Before Justine could move towards the tea tray, the double doors at the rear of the large open space banged open to reveal a line of five porters carrying 'Green 10'. It was in three separate pieces, the smallest of the three was the one so nearly dropped when the couriers collected it from the studio. Justine had brought her installation kit which covered most eventualities - paints, glue, Blu-Tack, pins, assorted brushes, knives and scissors plus a bottle of Rescue Remedy drops. In her experience there was usually a need for the latter at some point during the opening two days of an exhibition, either for herself or someone else on the team who was verging on hysterics or depression. Generally she preferred to handle her work herself, to watch it being wrapped, transported, unwrapped and assembled by a stranger must feel as Mr Rubik felt when watching someone attempt his cube for the first time. The nuts and bolts of fitting it together were to her mind straightforward, but after all these years Justine still disliked that moment when it all came together in case she looked at it and knew it was wrong, even though it had looked perfectly fine in her studio. She had learned to accept that some pieces may never be finished to her satisfaction, and that her endless fiddling with them didn't help.

To defer looking at the porters as they worked, she took a biscuit. A shortbread fan, her favourite. She preferred the thin crispiness of the fan to the chunkier bite of a finger. One hundred per cent butter, of course. She chewed and remembered Christmas, so many Christmases, her mother and the 1953 Coronation biscuit tin. The tin now sat on her desk back at the studio, having been brought back to London by Justine after the funeral. It was empty. She planned to fill it with shortbread and keep it next to her kettle as an alternative to chocolate. A belated recognition that her chocolate consumption may aggravate her headaches.

The porters assembled 'Green 10' correctly. It required a small fleck of Prussian Green on one corner, smudged and blended. The particular rag in her kit today had once been a white designer t-shirt and, as she dabbed, she remembered a three-way argument in Malaga with April and Catalina about what type of cloth constituted the best rag. April said it was an old tea towel, one of the white ones with a blue or green stripe which your granny used for polishing glasses. For Catalina, a neatly hemmed square cut from an old brushed cotton bed sheet. The pattern didn't matter, she insisted. Justine had argued that any type of rag should do the job and she still thought so. It was just that the quality of cotton of her worn-out t-shirts now was organic Egyptian not economy grade with the odd cotton seed woven in as it had been in Malaga.

It was 30 years since that discussion took place in the apartment at Plaza de la Merced and she was ashamed to say she had no idea where Catalina was now. April was living in Barcelona and writing for an art website called *Gallery*. Definitely still the April that Justine remembered, quick to give feedback to everyone else but prickly to suggestions that her own work could be improved. They had sat late into the summer nights on that tiny balcony in Malaga, enjoying the cooling of the night air as Spaniards do, living their lives outside at night like a trio of bats. The three girls imagined their future art careers, discussed endlessly the merits of Miró versus Picasso versus Dalí versus Velazquez. They argued about the point at which they would justifiably be able to call themselves 'artist' – selling their first piece, being interviewed for *Artforum*, showing at the Biennale, being made a Royal Academician, making their first million, seeing their work on permanent display at a major museum like the Tate or the Prado.

She circled 'Green 10', rag in hand, adding a green smudge here and there, none really essential but grateful for having something practical to do and excusing her from the small talk. Zuzannah and Maud's heads were bent together like two courting swans. From Thursday onwards her days would be full of small talk. Now she just wanted to head home. She thought of the squashy sofa awaiting her, how comfortable it would feel to sit there alone in the sitting room surrounded by quiet, her eyes closed, her mind still.

She closed her eyes. Tonight she might cook spaghetti bolognese for supper and let Darya choose a DVD they could watch together. Tomorrow she was not needed here so she could potter in her studio, pack away her 'Green' materials and lay all her work surfaces bare. Perhaps attempt to remove the worst of the Brilliant White spillage from her studio floor, if she had the energy. She would dust the shelves and if the day was fine she would wash the windows and throw them open to let in the weak February daylight. She would deal with the tower of unopened post in the black plastic tray on her desk, sort through the 1500 or so e-mails in her inbox, answer the cards and notes of sympathy.

Tomorrow she would take a fresh view on the world, a view that wasn't green. At the thought of embarking on a new project, exploring, researching, playing with a new subject, she opened her eyes again to the moment. She licked her lips and removed every trace of shortbread biscuit.

Tomorrow, she would fill her mother's tin.

Post Natal compression

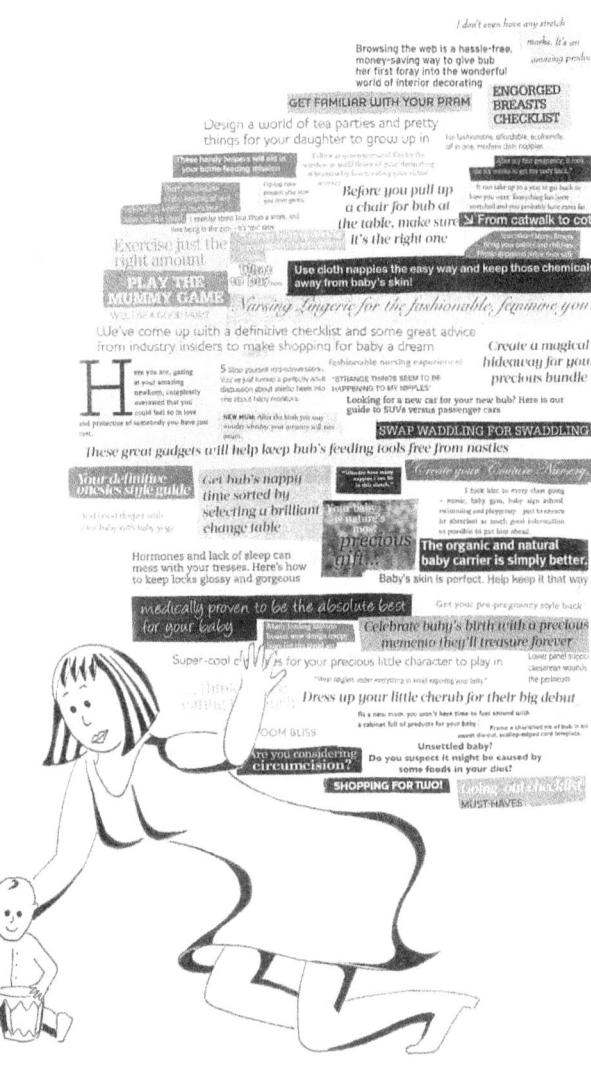

money-saving way to give bub her first foray into the wonderful world of interior decorating

amazing product

GET FAMILIAR WITH YOUR PRAM

ENGORGED BREASTS CHECKLIST

Design a world of tea parties and pretty things for your daughter to grow up in

For fashionable, affordable, ecofriendly, all in one, modern cloth nappies.

These handy helpers will aid in your bottle-feeding mission

Yellow or green curtains? Cot by the window or wall? Solve all your decorating dilemmas by first creating your virtual nursery

"After my first pregnancy, it took me six weeks to get my body back."

There's nothing like a baby's bottom on your gift a dent in that skin in the breast.

Flip-top cover protects your little one from germs.

Before you pull up a chair for bub at the table, make sure it's the right one

It can take up to a year to get back to how you were. Everything has been stretched and you probably have extra fat.

I exercise about four times a week, and love being in the gym – it's 'me' time

↘ **From catwalk to cot**

Chipped, cheedy or rubbed in, a reasonable style with a plain

Specialised Mum: fitness. Bring your babies and children. Physio approved pelvic floor safe.

cise just the amount

AY THE MY GAME

What to buy…

Use cloth nappies the easy way and keep those chemicals away from baby's skin!

A GOOD MUM?

Nursing Lingerie for the fashionable, feminine you!

ome up with a definitive checklist and some great advice ustry insiders to make shopping for baby a dream

Create a magical hideaway for your precious bundle

fashionable nursing experience!

you are, gazing ur amazing born, completely awed that you d feel so in love ebody you have just

5 Stop yourself mid-conversation. You've just turned a perfectly adult discussion about stiletto heels into one about baby monitors.

"STRANGE THINGS SEEM TO BE HAPPENING TO MY NIPPLES"

NEW MUM: After the birth you may wonder whether your memory will ever return.

Looking for a new car for your new bub? Here is our guide to SUVs versus passenger cars

SWAP WADDLING FOR SWADDLING

t gadgets will help keep bub's feeding tools free from nasties

ive e guide

Get bub's nappy time sorted by selecting a brilliant change table

with y yoga

"Wonder how many nappies I can fit in this clutch."

Your baby is nature's most precious gift…

Create your Couture Nursery…

I took him to every class going – music, baby gym, baby sign school, swimming and playgroup – just to ensure he absorbed as much good information as possible to put him ahead

The organic and natural baby carrier is simply better.

mones and lack of sleep can ss with your tresses. Here's how keep locks glossy and gorgeous

Baby's skin is perfect. Help keep it that way

edically proven to be the absolute best or your baby ♥

Get your pre-pregnancy style back

Many leading fashion houses now design nappy bags for dresses and tea

Celebrate baby's birth with a precious memento they'll treasure forever

Super-cool costumes for your precious little character to play in

Lower panel supports caesarean wounds and the perineum

"Wear singlets under everything to avoid exposing your belly."

Dress up your little cherub for their big debut

…think you're eating too much

As a new mum, you won't have time to fuss around with a cabinet full of products for your baby.

BABY ROOM BLISS

Frame a cherished pic of bub in this sweet die-cut, scallop-edged card template.

Unsettled baby? Do you suspect it might be caused by some foods in your diet?

Are you considering circumcision?

SHOPPING FOR TWO!

Going out checklist

MUST-HAVES

Fresh eyes
by Kasia James

My child remakes me a traveler
The invisible familiar
made exotic
by first experience

Raising a Mom in a Dozen Observations
or Kids raise their Moms and other things no one told me about motherhood
by Sabrina Garie

You get the kid you get

My daughter wears hats—sequined berets, spangled fedoras, bejewelled baseball caps. If it sparkles and shines she'll put it on her head and rock it, then coordinate it with suspenders, half gloves, belts, layered tops or just the right pair of earrings. And shoes. Of course, shoes. Once, she forgot to dress up for photo day so she ripped her shirt to make it more interesting.

When I arrive at my parent-teacher meeting every year, I spend four of my allotted 15 minutes discussing her fashion. The teachers always bring it up.

I've always wondered why she does. I don't own hats. Stylish is not one of the things my friends would accuse me of being. No one around her puts them on. That sense of style is uniquely her own.

Kids leave the womb with a good chunk of their personalities fully formed, like Athena jumping out of Zeus's head. Mythology has so many life lessons hidden in its images. My little Athena's personality shone from birth—attention hungry, queasy stomach, independent as all heck, total foodie, nap resistant, talkaholic, in total control of her world, and dressed herself as soon as she possibly could. I've been running to catch up ever since she arrived.

Kids raise their moms

When my child was born (not that long ago since time speeds up once children take over your life), I had this crazy impression—a total dream—that I would tell her what to do and of course, bowing to my wisdom and not insignificant life experience, she'd just do it. Because kids do what parents tell them.

And so I told her, and then I told her again, and again. When I looked in the mirror, a nagging shrew looked back at me. My progeny never blossomed under the words of my great wisdom, especially when said (maybe shouted) repeatedly.

Lo and behold, she had her own ideas about what she should do and how things should go. She wasn't always right, but boy she was insistent and persistent (I could use the word annoying here but I won't go there).

Since telling didn't work, I took a lesson from writing and decided to start showing. Gandhi nailed it. "Be the change you want to be."

No wonder my kid could be annoying: I was a mess. My manners had disintegrated into the toilet, my telephone number must be plastered on the dart board of the rec room in several phone centres worldwide, sugar took up too many of my daily calories, work stress was eating through me from the inside out and I bitched about my evil landlord incessantly.

My dad practiced the "do as I say, not as I do" model of parenting. It doesn't work. I was too smart for that, so is my daughter. So my real work began, of learning to raise myself better, to be a more effective mom.

I followed her lead. Laugh more, play more, engage more, use crayons and pictures, not always words. To raise my child, I had to learn to reconnect with my inner child, who had retreated so long ago in the face of work, parenthood, bills, and the accumulation of life's pain.

My diet also changed, my sharing-of-wisdom lectures shortened to tweets, I found a better job, we moved to a nicer house. I still chew out robotic call centre workers, just less often.

Ego push-ups required

Kids can be just plain mean. How many times have I heard "You're really bad at that mom," or "Mom, you can never, ever, ever, ever wear a bikini." Or maybe she just sits down next to me and starts to count the grey hairs on the back of my head. The ones I can't see so I don't have to acknowledge that they exist.

Even with a solid ego, it rankles. Age and responsibility start taking things away, making it harder to be and do what I once was and could. Now, I hear all about it in cold, stark detail.

So ego push-ups every day rank high on my morning routine. If I don't tell myself how awesome I am, I won't hear it much. It helps. If you are doing your absolute best to raise your kid, you are awesome. By definition. By choice. By design. I promise. Now you say it. "I'm awesome."

Not tiger mom and proud

It's not just the kids who think they've got a monopoly on what moms should be doing. Society at large feels it has every right to tell me how to be a mom. Yes, they are implying that I'm not being a good one—to sell products, to make themselves right, and just because they can.

Look at the sheer number of parenting books, magazines and blogs. Whatever you feel about tiger mom (and I'm not going there either), it's marketed as a way to tell us moms we aren't doing it right by our kids. All we have to do is buy the book and, viola, we'll know how to raise that perfect kid who plays violin and goes to Harvard or maybe Yale. If your child doesn't, well…. Between my own head and my kid, I don't need any more grief.

Tiger mom's claim to expertise is that she is, well, she's a…mom. Which means she's an expert on parenting her kids. For my child, I am the only one who can claim expertise, and that's chancy at best. Just when I think I know her, wham bam it changes on me ma'am.

Everything always changes

Every time I blink, my kid transforms—can do something she couldn't, has a new characteristic, sees the world through a new set of lenses. It's like stepping into a transporter and instantly going from one place in the relationship to another. One day she needs a push to swing on a swing. The next day, her feet reach the clouds all on her own initiative.

Other times there are markers, indicators that a subtle shift has occurred, a blurring of formerly understood roles and rules, the opening of a whole new door. With these, I watch my perspective, even my world view unravel and then re-knit itself and I'm forced to let go of something—an assumption, a belief, "a fact". Here are some of my markers, so you can see them. You'll have your own.

- The first time she held a bottle by herself and started to feed herself was my first kick in the pants as to how quickly she wasn't going to need me anymore.

- When she slammed her bedroom door because she was angry with me to retake control after she lost it. My babe has a temper, I'm still learning to manage around it. Huffing into her room and door slamming morphed into one of the dances on our mom-kid dance card.

- The first sleepover, a physical sign of her moving away from me, into herself, toward her friends.

- She lied to me and then told me about it, exploring her own moral lines, what she can get away with, what she wants to get away with. Kids are pretty bad liars—at first. As she gets better, I become a smarter lie detector.

- Asked about sex and the first time I answered her. They were not the same time. The question came much earlier than I expected and I was not prepared. The outside world comes in fast and furious and I wasn't ready. I'm often not.

- Made me laugh when I was being grumpy and took the initiative to make the environment friendlier. There are some real upsides to her growing independence. She has become a real person to hang out with. We even like the same movies, finally.

- Cleaned up without me asking. Responsibility as habit not theory.

- Planned her entire birthday party including some budgeting. She grows daily into her own skills and needs mine less.

- Swatted me away because I was embarrassing her. That's when I perfected the 'evil mom' laugh.

- Stayed home by herself. As many things are, this was harder on me than her.

Hoard credit cards and nab an accounting degree

Kids do horrible things to your wallet. Dance lessons, music lessons, sports teams, uniforms, new or new-to-you clothes every year, academic enhancement, braces, refilling the gas tank in between all the commuting to and fro and monthly injections to the college fund.

That's just from the kid themselves. Society comes back at you demanding brightly packaged, socially expected, community-mandated milestones with ever increasing price tags. Birthday parties (and the content of those goody bags), gift-bearing holidays, rites of passage such as bar-mitzvahs, communions, graduations (which now start at pre-K), sweet sixteens and quincineras. Weddings and college still to come.

Managing costs and debt means managing credit cards and mastering excel spreadsheets. Switching balances around, getting new ones, finding interest free options, keeping track. I would always think—once I no longer have to pay for day care, it will get easier. Once I don't have to pay for before and after care, it will get easier. But something always comes along to its place in my monthly accounting balance.

I started buying lottery tickets, something I've never done. Just in case.

Hell is other parents

Other people can bring out the worst in you. Not just magazines and tiger mom books. Parenting gets competitive. I preened my feathers with the best of them when my daughter was chosen for a competitive gymnastics team. I learned fast how to boast, without boasting, brag without bragging. It's so simple, it's scary. You ask about another child to open up the space for you to let loose. When my kid didn't do so well, I had a back pocket full of reasons why - she's younger than most of the other team kids, not enough sleep, juggling school and gymnastics etc... Someone has to be best, so I held out for my kid. Why not? Because it made me icky.

I'm ashamed to admit, it got worse for a while. When my babe performed and got her score, the only thing between her and the medal is another girl's performance. I confess. I wished the other children competing would do not do well—pull a landing or step out of the lines or just perform badly—so mine could win. Once I did it, I had to struggle not do it again. Perfectly understandable, many would say in sympathy, because I know they do the same thing. I sit next to them on the bleachers.

Damn. I'm guilty of wishing a child ill so my child could what? Get a medal or a ribbon.

Once I conquered the competitive mom trap, my daughter left gymnastics for dance and recitals. Why is she in the back line? Shouldn't she be in the front?

Mainlining pride fixes

Even when she's the dancer in the back row, my emotions get all gloppy and my cheeks ache from smiling. Just like my chest puffs out when I watch my little one screech that trumpet, the only girl trumpeter in the in the band, or at the plays and songs she writes, her ability to needle me into a better mood, her competence at organizing her own birthday parties, the way she fiercely defends her friends from all naysayers, that she's been planning her campaign for student government presidency for over a year, and I can keep going and going and going.

I've gotten addicted to those pride infusions.

Like my daughter, I did gymnastics too, was on the high school team but never really prospered with it. She made it to the national championships, has a drawer full of medals and ribbons by the age I had mastered a cartwheel.

When she decided to quit, I was devastated. I made her stick it out for a while longer just to be sure. She was. I wasn't.

I still miss her gymnastics. She never looks back. That's when I had to admit, I was living out my unrealized childhood dreams through her. It's me, not her, that went through withdrawal. It was me, not her, who wanted to go the distance. I lost a boost to my own ego when I all did was sit in those damn uncomfortable bleachers (ugh), pay for the lessons (ouch), and cheer my heart out (pass me a throat lozenge please).

I'd do it all over again.

Watch from the shadows, steal the credit in the light

It's not like I did any of those wonderful things I tend to preen about. Her talents and traits may stem from genetic material donated by an obscure medieval ancestor from the paternal side of the family. It might be an idea she took from a book she read in school.

I encourage, support, applaud, listen, and talk to her even when she's not listening or writing on the walls, stuffing the cat into costumes and then crying when she get scratched. Sometimes the best support I can give her is to let her blossom on her own.

She's the one that chooses out the hats, wears them, accessorizes them, and rocks them. Me, I drive to Target, veto the expensive ones and swipe the credit card.

Then, like any good politician in my neighbourhood (I live in Washington, D.C.) I grab the credit.

Aspirin works for shadow pain

My wanting my kid to win is not as shallow as it sounds—at least not all of it. Part of loving her is feeling what she feels. I never, ever want her to hurt, even though I know I can't protect her from most of it.

Growing up hurts and I get to do it all over again, through my daughter. Motherhood seems to bring on its own unique version of shadow pain—feeling the limb that is no longer there. A psychic emotional chord drags me into my kid's trauma, forces me to relive my own adolescent angst again. My daughter came home one day in tears because a friend stabbed her in the back. I remembered being alone on the elementary school playground in my favourite blue checkered dress I wore with the red and blue harlem globe trotters sneakers when I bawled over the same thing.

Aspirin works for shadow pain. Wine works better. Scotch works best.

A childhood relived is one relieved

With ever tear that I cry with my daughter, an internal wound also heals.

That lesson took hold at the elementary school spring fair while I watched her scurry up the climbing wall. Flexible arms and legs easily reaching from hand hold to hand hold, foot hold to foot hold. Envy was a drumbeat in my blood. That used to be me, easing my way to the sky. Until childbirth left me no time, life insurance ramped up the costs for extreme sport enthusiasts, and my body didn't work quite as well. Me aside, my pride in her lifted with every confident reach, with every inch she ascended. My daily pride fix.

Until she looked down.

Her fear of heights beat down her love of climbing and sent her rappelling to the ground, unwilling to finish even though she was more than capable of doing so.

Although every cell in my body wished her to look back up, to continue to climb, to overcome the anxiety, I understood. That also used to be me.

So many things I didn't finish or gave up on because I was afraid. I spent my first two decades running away and every one since then learning to manage the fear, so it didn't become a steel barrier to the quality of my life and the height of my aspirations. Step by step, I learned how to get out of my own way.

So when the fear showed up in her, I knew she didn't get it from watching me. It's just part of the programming.

Finally, I understood in that gut-wrenching, life-twisting way, that my not-so-great childhood and early adulthood may not have been because there was something wrong with me. Raising my kid is like reliving my childhood, but through the eyes of an adult. While painful, it is also cathartic, a release of so much past angst.

And I'm very glad, I'm not doing it again, for real.

You are the mom you are

Perhaps my greatest disappointment was that motherhood didn't change me enough. I knew, I just knew, that as a mom I would arise above my petty fears and inhibitions, be something I really wasn't, in the name of my child. Motherhood was the quick route to achieving perfection. Of course I'd be able to control my moods and display extreme patience with my child under any circumstance. I'd never raise my voice, nag, take out my work stress on her or show my fears to her - not me, never me. The list, unfortunately, goes on. It's a load of crock. I have failed on every single count. Because I'm stuck with me, child or not.

There are days when my Herculean (or perhaps I should say Amazonian) efforts do merit a Wonder Woman costume (complete with truth lasso and invisible plane). But in the end, I'm my own person, my daughter is hers. Family is about love, support and the sharing of joy and sorrow but internal growth for both mom and the kid, remains rooted in self. It comes from within, from the choices each of us makes about who we are, what we value, and how we want to live. Parenthood changed some of my priorities, but not all. Nor should it.

I am who I am. I'm going make it good and love the kid I've got because she is who she is.

I'll conclude with a question I've learned to ask myself every day. It's not 'Who do I want my kid to be?' I want only that she is herself and that she is happy and good and fulfilled. The question that I wake up to every morning is 'What kind of mom do I want to be?'

Parents like Amy Chua are the reason why Asian-Americans like me are in therapy
by Betty Ming Liu

On Jan. 8, 2011, The Wall Street Journal published an essay entitled, 'Why Chinese Mothers are Superior.' It was an excerpt from "The Battle Hymn of the Tiger Mom," a new memoir by a Yale University Law School professor, Amy Chua. As the American-born daughter of immigrants of Chinese descent, Chua proudly declared herself a Tiger Mom who was raising her two daughters as top students and accomplished musicians. Her secret? Taking total control over their lives. They studied hard, practiced hard; playdates and sleepovers were banned. This was how Chua's tiger parents raised her and she was carrying on family tradition.

Within hours, an international debate on parenting techniques took off with return fire from another American-born daughter of Chinese tiger parents who is also a professor and mother. By the afternoon of Jan. 8, 2011, her catchy headline was catching on too: "Parents like Amy Chua are the reason Asian-Americans like me are in therapy." The post went viral as readers, finding an outlet for their collective fury, linked to it on Facebook and Twitter.

The blogger, Betty Ming Liu, is a New York University journalism professor and a single, divorced mom. In her blog post, she spelled out how her "control freak" parents left her with a diminished sense of self that was only recovered through years of therapy, a divorce and career changes. In raising her own daughter, she blogged that her goals are to focus on what she never had: Unconditional love and a clear shot at personal happiness.

To this day, the blog post on BettyMingLiu.com continues to draw comments from tiger parenting survivors from around the world. Hundreds of readers have left their personal stories of depression, suicide and just plain miserable childhoods. Meanwhile, a thoughtful, serious discussion keeps expanding with the publication of evermore fresh research on tiger parenting's negative impact. Other writers have also responded with published accounts of their own experiences, some in favour but most against the unnecessary pain inflicted by parental tough love.

The full blog post is reprinted below and stands as the first call for a serious reflection on what it means to love our children when we - no matter what our race, colour or creed — have been raised by mothers and fathers who can best be described as tiger parents.

....

All day long, people have been telling me about an article headlined: "Why Chinese Mothers Are Superior." And I've had enough! I'm posting my reaction so that I don't have to keep talking about it. Getting to the point: the piece is crap. But its writer, Yale Law School Professor Amy Chua, is also a marketing genius. Let me explain....

The article ran in this morning's Wall Street Journal. It's an excerpt from her memoir, which hits book stores on Tuesday. With everyone in the Asian American community jabbering about it, she and publisher Penguin Press are getting tons of free publicity for "Battle Hymn of the Tiger Mother."

If, like me, you've never heard of this woman, don't worry. The Wikipedia.org entry about her is oh-so-current. Yes, it just happens to have a link to today's shrewdly-timed Journal article. Hmmm.

As for the actual piece, all I can say is that Chua is a narrow-minded, joyless bigot. Don't waste your money on the book. I'll even spare you the drudgery of reading her essay by giving you highlights from the Journal excerpt:

Chua begins by explaining that the reason "Chinese parents raise such stereotypically successful kids" is because the children are totally controlled. She doesn't let her kids do sleepovers, have playdates, be in school plays, watch TV or mess with computer games.

Her two daughters are also forbidden from choosing their own extracurricular activities. They have to be the top students in every subject except gym and drama. They must bring home A's.

Kids need to be relentlessly drilled to achieve. "What Chinese parents understand is that nothing is fun until you're good at it," she writes. By the way, taking piano and violin lessons are a must.

This overachieving — and overreaching — author writes about the time her father inspired her to excellence by telling her that she was "garbage." A proud product of her upbringing, she once mentioned at a dinner party that she had, in the past, called her own daughter Sophia "garbage" — to the child's face. Ugh.

....

There is a photo of Chua and her kids in The Wall Street Journal article, a self-congratulatory essay that goes on and on. You get the idea. Chua buys into the hardcore, traditional Chinese approach to tough love.

This is so sad because we're talking about values that have nearly ruined so many of us.

Of course, what's really sad is that Chua is perpetuating very dangerous ideas:

Haven't we had enough of over-pressured, guilt-ridden Asian immigrant and Asian-American college students committing suicide and acting out?

Who gave her the right to define what is means to be 'real' Chinese? Do all Chinese people have to behave like this to be authentic?

If you look at the Wall Street Journal photo of her daughters, they still look like girls to me. Isn't it frighteningly premature of her to hold them up as examples of her success? Would a good mother really behave like this?

I know casual observers will think Chua knows what she's talking about because she teaches at Yale, and is a graduate of both Harvard College (magna cum laude) and Harvard Law School.

Well, there's a dirty little secret about these lunatic, prestige-whoring Chinese parents that Chua represents. For all their lusting after the elitism of Ivy League degrees, what they admire more than anything is financial success. So on that note, I would like to recommend a different book for you to read: *Delivering Happiness: A Path to Profits, Passion, and Purpose*.

A dear friend recently gave me a copy and I'm enjoying every page of it. This bestseller has been #1 on both The New York Times and Wall Street Journal lists. Even more than that, *'Delivering Happiness'* was the most popular gift book item for 2010, according to Publishers Weekly.

This memoir by Tony Hsieh tells how he co-founded the Internet company LinkExchange. He sold it in 1999 for $265 million, when he was 24. Later, he went on to help grow the Zappos.com footwear website into a $1 billion company. Along the way, he revolutionized the shoe business. Oh my goodness, he's only in his mid-30s!

....

Like Chua, he's also the American-born child of immigrants of Chinese heritage (his parents are from Taiwan). He writes about being a kid who was forced to play four musical instruments and pressured to study hard. Like Chua, he went to Harvard, too.

But read the book. The young man had fun! I found his memoir inspiring — and not just because he's made money while I'm still sitting around counting my tiny stacks of George Washingtons.

I am in awe of people who get outside the box to do something different, something creative and original. Tony — may I call him Tony? — has a fabulous story. He didn't submit to the browbeating of parental values and immigrant culture. Instead, he took chances, fumbled and made mistakes. That, in turn, gave him the wisdom to trust his personal vision.

But getting back to Chua's essay. In it, she writes: "I'm happy to be the one hated."

Poor thing. It's the only time the word 'happy' appears in this excerpt from her book.

As for me, I'm happy to be the one…who is finally happy. I sucked at piano, which my mother made me study because she had been a child too poor for lessons. My grades in college were so bad that one semester, I had a straight D average. Screwing up academically was the only power I had over my dad, a tyrant who wouldn't let me take art or English courses.

I'll spare you the rest…for now. You can read more details someday in my memoir. Haha.

Anyway, that's my rant for tonight. Don't bother with Chua. Instead, let us go on, with tenderness for ourselves and our children. Let us explore the joys of having a real life.

The bricklayer's daughter
by Laura Evans

The bricklayer's daughter does not fear the night. Why should she? The night is a friend to those who try not to be seen. She has practised sliding through shadows, rippleless, undetected. She can go where she wants.

Her father is protective; she is pretty. But her mother, who was also pretty once, leaves the key beneath the butter dish before she goes to bed. Her daughter has learnt to step in time with the city, not its sluggish daytime heartbeat but strange and relentless after-dark rhythms.

She watches the princess's suitors and is glad she is a bricklayer's daughter.

Full of abundance and feeling heavy
by Jessica Kennedy

I was in a hurry,
walking fast and rushed.
I had just left the house in slight chaos and was feeling unbalanced.
I had my baby boy strapped to my chest and was heading towards the public library to attend a parenting workshop.

I was feeling a little 'heavy' and weighed down.
The physical weight of the baby and my canvas bag filled with the necessities needed to successfully attend a two hour workshop with an infant were burying deep within the muscles of shoulders and back.

I had just shut the door to my house, leaving a trail of chaos. My thoughts still back there, wondering if my husband remembered the very intricate
and unnecessary bedtime routine for two
very spirited toddlers.
My worries were substantial.

The emotional weight of the rushed night and busy day were bearing heavy on my mind.
I was feeling good but exhausted.

I felt as though I was balancing on a tight-rope hoping not to fall in a pit of self defeat.
One slip of my footing and I could easily spiral from 'strong mama' to 'broken woman'.

I didn't want to be late.
I just couldn't move fast enough.
I chose to take a shortcut.

I walked along the path of the old rail road tracks.
I walked across the bridge and looked in on the waterfront condominiums.
These homes have windows from ceiling to floor, allowing the residents to have full access to the beauty of the Mississippi.

As I unabashedly peered into these windows, I drank in the brief snap shots of the lives of others.
I interpreted my pictures into a full collage of what life was like in these homes.

I saw adult homes.
Beautiful art.
Clean kitchens.
Adult conversations.
Hot meals at appropriate times.

In the dimmed lights of a living room I saw a woman sitting comfortably on the couch watching the news.
And for a brief moment, I wished that was me.
I wished I was alone on my couch watching the news.
In silence, living my adult life amongst beautiful art and drinking tea in a clean kitchen.

But it didn't take long for me to fall back into reality.
The slow and rhythmical breathing of my sweet baby boy against my own chest reminded me.

Reminded me that even with the chaos, I didn't want to be anywhere else.
His little heart beat against mine reminded me what it felt like to not be alone.
I wanted to admire my babies' paintings as great works of art.
I wanted to sing Old McDonald for the 100th time.
I wanted to eat dinner at 4:30 pm so I can make sure they get to bed early and have a restful night.
I wanted to sit messy kitchen nursing a baby amongst princess playing cards and children's sippy cups.
I wanted to enjoy my cold cup of tea.
I wanted my life.

The weight of my busy and chaotic days may make me feel heavy,
but the weight of my babies on my soul makes me feel plentiful.

The intense substance of my life keeps me grounded.
Keeps me here.
Allowing me to feel full of abundance and heavy.

Mama Spider's Sacrifice
by Angélique Jamail

One Saturday last autumn, I spent the early morning pulling weeds from my hopeless flower beds before some friends came over and could see just how terrible a gardener I am. My husband was mowing the lawn. Late September had sucked the energy of summer's heat out of the air and left a brilliant blue sky overhead and zephyrs near the ground. I was enjoying the obvious sense of accomplishment derived from the industry of yanking loosely tethered starbursts of unintended grasses and chickweed from the mulch between the rosebushes. Another handful into the trash bag, and another, and another, and here, two or three handfuls at once. Soon I'd filled the bag and dropped it into the bin at the curb before the garbage truck came by. Double achievement.

I pulled my gloves off and wandered inside to get another bag, checking on my six-year-old daughter on my way through the house. She'd been watching cartoons on television - alone, because her four-year-old brother had gone on his first sleepover at his best friend's house the night before and not come home yet - but she was now more engrossed in writing a story about three orphaned kittens adopted by a princess named Cherry Blossom. I smiled approvingly at her and tried not to giggle. The day before, she'd told me she wanted to change her name to Cherry Blossom and then asked if we could get a new cat for Christmas to keep our elderly one company. I'd told her she could do both, if she still really wanted to, when she turned eighteen. Writing a story about it was her stopgap. In the kitchen I poured myself a glass of cold water, drank it, then plodded numbly to the mudroom where we keep the trash bags. Halfway through the doorway, I stopped.

On the floor, mere inches from our cat's food dish, was a large spider. Its brownish legs were splayed out in a crouch, its mottled gray body the size, realistically, of a nickel. I didn't get my face too close, but I thought it was a weird looking spider, not the usual wolves or orbs we typically see around our home. I walked calmly back to the cabinet where we keep glass vases and empty jars and pulled a mason jar from the shelf; then I walked calmly back toward the spider and enclosed it under glass.

I want to make perfectly clear that I did not freak out.

I did not scream or cry or scratch the skin of my arms until they bled. I did not pull my hair or run from the room. I did not try to squash the bug with a very heavy book or sic my husband's aging feline on it. I did not drop a brick on the spider. Despite my history of arachnophobia (which I have *mostly* conquered), I didn't even try to scoot the spider out of my house with a long-handled dustpan. Even though any of these scenarios might have been appropriate, my daughter was in the next room; I had to hold it together.

I peered more closely at the spider, though the jar distorted the image, and walked back into the living room to tell my daughter, in a very even and not at all frantic tone, it was there, lest she happen upon the beast herself and decide to remove the jar for a closer look. I envisioned the horror of the spider leaping onto her leg or arm or stomach, my daughter screaming, my husband and me being outside and unaware of the entire ordeal, the ensuing spider bites and trip to the emergency room and horrified fear of all eight-legged creatures planting itself within her young mind, leading to a lifetime of being unable to sweep even the tiniest bug from the corners of her bathroom.

That's no way to rear a child.

"Honey," I said to her, "there's a big spider in the kitchen under a glass jar. Please leave it alone."

"Okay, Mama," she said then jumped up. "I want to see it!"

We went back to the doorway of the mudroom and she peered curiously at the spider, while I retrieved a trash bag for weeding the garden and peered at her out of the corner of my eye to make sure she didn't touch the jar.

"That sure is a big bug!" she exclaimed.

"Sure is," I said, ushering her back to the living room. "Let's give it some privacy, okay?" She nodded cheerfully and sat down in front of her cartoon, in front of her pencil and journal, and got happily back to work.

I went outside and walked up to my husband, who was still cutting the grass. When he saw me, he turned off the mower.

"I just wanted you to know there's a spider the size of a chihuahua in the kitchen under a mason jar." I was very matter-of-fact about the whole thing. "I've already told Hannah to stay away from it."

He smiled, used to my fear. "I'll go take care of it," he said, heading toward the house.

"Whenever you have a moment," I said casually.

I'd finished weeding the garden by the time he finally emerged from the front door, jar full of spider in hand. Hannah was close on his heels, anxiously peering around the side of his hip at the spectacle he was carrying.

"It's a mother wolf spider," he explained, "and it's dying. Its babies are all over it." He began to empty the jar into the ferns near the front door.

"Not there!" I said. I pointed to the far corner of the house, a good thirty feet from the front gate. He took the jar back to the shady corner and emptied the no doubt zillions of tiny too-many-legged monsters into the grass. When he came back, he described what appeared to him to be the weaning process. Apparently the babies hatch and then consume the mother, leaving her large husk on the floor as they make their creepy little ways into the world. "Yikes," I murmured, feeling both terror and understanding. "I guess that's why the body looked gray and mottled."

"Yeah, those were the babies. I saw a little spider walking near the big one and thought it was odd, because normally, you know, spiders don't like other spiders to come near them. Then I took a closer look." He shrugged. "Nature's funny. With black widows, they consume the father."

I shuddered as he walked back inside, and Hannah ran to me and hugged me, tears welling up in her dark brown eyes. "They're eating their mommy?" she asked.

I sighed. "So it would seem," I said gently. Then we walked awkwardly back into the house, her clinging to me, sobbing, while I tried to comfort her, explaining that this must be the way their species does things, and that the mama spider was very willing to make this sacrifice, and that she loved her babies very, very much, and that they were all going to be happy and healthy because of it. Eventually, my daughter calmed down and went back to her journal. I could only imagine what was going to happen next in the story of Princess Cherry Blossom and her adopted kittens.

I then tried to finish cleaning up the garden and driveway before it got any later.

Afterward as I was taking a shower, frantically trying to clean up myself before our company came over, I thought about that life cycle. If that's really how it works in Wolf Spider Land – and this wasn't just some disgusting ambush playing out in the Spider House of Horrors – then it was hard not to conflate the spider babies with human ones, even just a little bit.

Certainly I love my children and would never trade them for anything, least of all the hobbies I willingly abandoned after they were born. But no matter how much we think we've prepared for it, children alter us, even permanently, in ways we can't always predict.

My own mother had just turned seventy the day before I found the spiders in my doorway. That weekend we were going to a party at her house; for the first time in so many years I couldn't remember how long, my mother was throwing herself a birthday party to celebrate her age rather than mourn it. *Finally,* I'd thought, shoving aside the looming dread of aging that often, since my children were born and the generation had turned itself over, threatened to take root inside of me. I tried to list off the hobbies my mother enjoys: mostly crafty pursuits, such as making pillows or little dresses for my daughter, decorating her beautiful house or making costumes for my sister and me. Things I don't remember her doing – or even being able to do – when I was growing up. Back then, her time was consumed by raising three children.

I deeply appreciate and admire my mother's sacrifices while we were growing up. I'm well aware of many of them, and I know that to list them here – even in tribute to her – would take up more space than people would read. But I wonder what's been lost. In her younger days, she was a cosmetics model and a computer programmer and a teacher. She drove a sporty little Grand Prix and took Judo and danced at discotheques on the weekends.

What will my children know about my life before them (and I mean "know" in a strictly theoretical sense)? What about my youth will seem so outrageously out of character, according to their understanding of me, that it will seem as if that younger person's existence belonged to someone else, a stranger or a character in a book, some ghostly husk of memory of a life that is no more?

When my son returned, late that morning, from his sleepover, he ran into the house and nearly knocked me down with a hug.

"How was your playdate?" I asked him.

"It was a blast!" he shouted, all enthusiasm and beaming smiles.

I sat down, and he climbed into my lap. Not to be left out, Hannah ran over and jumped on me too.

"I missed you," he said, grinning, wrapping his arms around my neck.

"I missed you, too!" Hannah insisted.

"But I've been right here with you," I said to her.

"Doesn't matter," she said and clung to me. Then they both began making playful mewling noises and kissing me all over my head. They knocked me over with their hugs. Liam began roaring like a dinosaur. I tickled him and his contagious laugh infected us all.

I hadn't swept the floor yet. I hadn't prepared the lunch. The doorbell was going to ring any minute.

I felt consumed.

Madre, hay una sola
by Judith Logan Farias

Failure of Heaven
by Christa Forster

Julianne Hernandez rocked back and forth on the hospital gurney, clutching her five-year-old son, who was stoned full of Benadryl and 160 ccs of epinephrine, against her breast. Alex seemed comatose in his tiger coat, part of the Halloween costume he'd worn for trick or treating earlier that evening. Julianne kept whispering questions into his ear – *how do you feel? Are you okay? Are you feeling better?*—waiting for signs of her son's return to normalcy. Alex kept his eyes open wide, but he seemed not to hear his mother's questions. Julianne worried that he might be brain damaged as a result of the anaphylactic shock, the reason for this trip to the emergency room to Texas Children's Hospital at 11 p.m. on Halloween.

The night nurse, an Asian man with kitty cat whiskers drawn over his smooth face, was gathering details from the EMTs who had ambulanced mother and child to the Emergency Room.

"Paediatric Caucasian male patient being admitted for observation after epinephrine injection to arrest anaphylactic shock." The tall black EMT leaned over the counter providing the night nurse with stats about time, amounts of medicine, skin colour.

"What caused his allergic reaction?" the nurse asked without looking at Julianne, pen poised above the admittance paperwork.

"Milk," the EMT answered.

"Goat's milk," Julianne clarified from the gurney.

"How was his colour when you arrived?" The nurse asked the EMT.

"He was blue," the EMT confirmed.

Julianne's heart swelled up against her ribcage.

"There was no known allergy to dairy before?" The night nurse said, turning his full attention toward Julianne.

"Not *this* bad."

The nurse looked concerned. "Who gave him the milk?" he asked.

"I did." Julianne said. She felt her chest flame with shame.

"We've got a room ready for your son, Mrs. Hernandez," an orderly dressed as an angel said. He unlocked the wheels of the gurney and nodded to the orderly on the other side - a devil - to begin rolling.

"How long do we need to stay here?" Julianne asked the angel.

"We have to observe him for at least six hours to make sure a paradoxical reaction to the epinephrine doesn't occur," he said.

"You okay?" the devil asked her.

"Paradoxical," Julianne said. "It's kind of funny you know, given your costumes?"

....

Julianne had taken Alex to a Halloween party at Cici Ferris's house. Cici, a new friend of Julianne's, was an oil heiress, a member of one of the founding families of Houston. She lived in a modern-style mansion on Del Monte in River Oaks, the Beverly Hills of Houston. Julianne sensed that Cici, whose own son had died almost one year to the day, was hosting this party for her friends as a way to deal with her own grief. She didn't know any of the other guests, and she felt awkward trying to talk to them. Most of them were immediate neighbours who lived in other mansions.

She had gone as Cindy Lauper; Alex, as a tiger. Leo Hernandez, Julianne's husband, stayed at home to work and hand out candy to the rare trick or treaters who knocked on the door of their unit in the condo complex.

The party was a hotdog/Tootsie Roll/Skittles fest, replete with pirates, princesses, dragons, one banana, one doctor, and one tiger. Upon returning from trick or treating on Cici's street, the kids dumped their candy into little piles before them to sort through their loot. Julianne sat next to Alex while he picked up each piece and held it out for her to confirm that it was safe for him to eat. Because Alex was severely allergic to most foods, Julianne confiscated the bulk of the candy. Later, she would "trade" Alex for it, replacing the Snickers, Three Musketeers, and Hershey's Kisses, piece for piece, with packets of gummi bears or individually-wrapped 86% dark chocolate squares. For the moment, he had to make do with the Smarties, the lollipops, the Pixie Sticks. She let him eat as many of these things as he wanted.

Near the end of the party, Julianne sat by herself on the floor of the pool house amidst the cloud of her crinoline skirt, watching "The Great Pumpkin" on the 70-inch plasma television. Alex appeared holding a real stethoscope.

"Where'd you find that?" Julianne asked.

"That kid," Alex pointed to tow-headed toddler dressed in blue scrubs with a blue paper surgeon's cap on his head.

"His parents must be doctors," Julianne said.

"Mommy, I need to check your heart,' Alex said.

She laughed as he climbed into her lap and touched her face with his hand and lips, as if feeling for a temperature. His hazel eyes looked to Julianne like a deep pond flecked by the swishes of fishes beneath the surface. She breathed deeply as he held the stethoscope against her chest.

"You're fine, Mommy," he said. "You're just fine," he repeated. "Everything is going to be okay."

"We're leaving in ten minutes," she called after him as he ran towards some kids playing air hockey in a corner of the pool house.

The lights of their porch were off when they arrived home, and Julianne suspected that Leo had not handed out one piece of candy while they were gone. Feeling physically wiped out, she offered Alex some real dinner – left-over organic chicken breast and sweet potato from the fridge – which he refused. She let Leo stay holed up in his office while she monitored Alex as he bathed, brushed his hair and teeth, and peed in the potty before getting into bed.

"Mommy?" Alex said.

She pulled the covers up around his neck. "It's sleepy time, Alex," she said.

"Can I have some milk?"

Normally, she would not have said yes, because Alex was still unaccustomed to getting up out of bed at night to go pee, but she went against her gut, rationalizing that he needed something besides sugar in his belly before sleep.

In the kitchen, she saw that they were out of rice milk. She reached in for the unopened carton of goat's milk. The naturopathic doctor overseeing Alex's dietary regime had recommended she start giving him probiotics to help improve and strengthen his digestion. She purchased the goat's milk to make yoghurt for Alex but had yet to do so. The milk's expiration stamp read 10-31. Even though it was bedtime, and a Friday evening, and even though in some distant corner of her body she sensed disaster, something else inside her said it would be okay to give him goat's milk. Just a couple tablespoons. Hadn't the naturopath said that goat's milk was a viable alternative for people who were allergic to cow's milk?

Alex gulped the goat's milk down without a fight. "I like it," he said with a smile, handing the empty red plastic cup back to her and snuggling down beneath his quilt. Julianne leaned down to kiss his forehead and smooth his hair back. She bid him good night and turned on the white noise machine and his soft, night-time music.

"See you in the morning, honey. I love you," she said from the doorway of his bedroom before pulling the door so that it was almost closed.

Ten minutes later from the back porch where she sat scrolling through emails on her phone, Julianne heard a hacking cough and screams coming from Alex's room. She jumped up and bolted into the house, dashing to Alex's room where she found her son curled up on the floor in front of his bed, scratching his arms to smithereens. His face was a rash of blistering hives, his lips swollen to twice their size. When he wasn't scratching his wrists, legs or face, Alex pulled on his tongue. He was coughing and coughing, struggling to breathe.

She scrambled to his side, dropping her cell phone on the wood floor, where it broke open, the battery skidding beneath the reading chair. She tried to pry Alex's hands away from his body to keep him from slicing open his skin with his fingernails.

"Leo!" Julianne screamed for her husband. "Alex, honey, try to relax—LEO!"

Leo appeared in the bedroom door, his iPod ear buds still in his ears.

"Get the Benadryl," Julianne yelled. "And call 911!" She'd never seen her son have a reaction like this: hives blistering out of the blue veins on his forehead, his lips so swollen they were about to burst, his rosy complexion waning from a dull gray into a faint blue.

"What?" Leo said, clearly confused.

"He's having an allergic reaction! Get the fucking Benadryl!"

"What did he eat?" Leo asked.

"Oh my *god*! Get the Benadryl or stay with him and I'll get the Benadryl," Julianne was hysterical now. Her energy combining with Alex's created a maelstrom of panic that threatened to explode open the room.

"Where is it?" Leo said.

"*Jesus Christ*," Julianne shouted. "Watch him!" She jumped up and hurled herself past her husband, knocking him hard into the doorjamb. She bee-lined to the kitchen where they kept medicines on the top shelf of a cabinet in a cardboard shoebox. She yanked the box out from the upper shelf, flipped it upside down so that all the bottles crashed onto the counter. She grabbed the Children's Liquid Benadryl, then rummaged frantically through the utensil drawer for a medicine dropper.

"Julianne!" Leo yelled, "Hurry up!"

"I am!" she screamed. She ran back to Alex's room. Leo was unsuccessfully trying to bear-hug Alex, as the child wheezed, rasped his wrists, and wrest what breath he could from his constricting airway.

"Here," Julianne shoved the medicine dropper and bottle into Leo's hands, "Give him one teaspoon. I can't see the numbers."

She knelt on the floor next to Alex and spoke in the most soothing tones she could muster, despite the pandemonium in her heart. "It's okay, honey, you're going to be okay. You're going to be okay. You're having an allergic reaction to the goat's milk. It's okay sweetie, try to relax." Leo helped Alex swallow the Benadryl, and the two of them waited with their writhing son as the miracle medicine started its work.

Julianne met Leo's eyes and felt a familiar accusatory glare.

"What?" Julianne asked.

"You gave him goat's milk?"

Ashamed and exhausted, Julianne felt her throat wring up, choking her ability to respond.

Within minutes, Alex's breathing steadied; his coughs became intermittent. The blistering hives receded into his veins. But his pallor remained gray. Julianne looked hard to see if he were regaining his color or losing even more of it. Alex swooned in and out of a conscious state.

"Keep him awake," Julianne croaked at Leo, as she reached under the reading chair, grabbed her cell phone battery and fumbled her phone back together in order to call 911.

....

Julianne Hernandez met Cici Ferris for the first time at Texas Children's Hospital, where one Monday, thinking it was a Tuesday, Julianne showed up for her Eczema Parents Support Group meeting and realized after ten minutes that she was in a support group for grieving families instead. Rather than leaving, she stayed in the meeting, riveted by prospect that it was possible for a child to die and leave behind these shredded souls, their parents. She didn't know how these people could even get out of bed to show up for this meeting. One of the parents in the group shared a story so horrifying, Julianne almost threw up while listening to it. This parent had lost her nine-month-old infant when her husband forgot to drop it off at daycare on his way to work downtown. The infant remained strapped in its car seat for seven hours in August, in a downtown parking garage. The child died from hyperthermia - heat exhaustion. The father hadn't even realized he'd forgotten the infant until he drove to the daycare to pick it up and it wasn't in the infant room. That's when he realized it was still in its car seat.

"He was shot," Cici noted flatly. They were sitting on one of the benches at Weir Park, watching Alex attempt to master the monkey bars.

"How?" Julianne gasped, relieved that Cici was talking about it because she'd been too scared to ask her about her son's death directly.

"With a shotgun," Cici continued. "He didn't die immediately. We were staying in our Sedona home, in Arizona. Louis had brought a friend with him, a boy – his oldest friend. We'd known him since the boys were in kindergarten together." Cici kept her eyes on the middle distance while she talked. "Tom - Tom and I were still together, of course - came into the backyard where the boys and I were playing checkers by the pool and announced that he'd seen a rattlesnake sunning itself on a rock at the edge of the property. He told Louis and Anders - the boy's name was Anders Anderson…." Cici trailed off for a moment. Julianne felt her own throat tighten, embarrassed by her mounting anxiety, guilty because her own very alive son was sprawled on the ground of the playground, letting the light breeze cool his sweaty face.

"Tom told them to go into the house and get the shotgun." Cici's voice snagged on a breath. Julianne wondered if Cici had ever told the story before, and she suspected from the halting tone that she might not have.

Before this moment, Julianne had invented her own version of how Louis had died: he choked on a grape; or, worse, he choked on a grape while Cici was in the other room reading her email. Or else, he died of a rare form paediatric pancreatic cancer. It had either been a sudden accident or else something terribly incurable, because Cici Ferris was rich enough, it seemed to Julianne, to stave off most of life's disasters. At least for a while. But this was the version of the story Julianne told herself before she knew that Louis had been thirteen when he died, too old to choke on a grape. Maybe. She'd revised the story so that it had thirteen year-old Louis drowning in the Ferris' pool. She never imagined it was a gun accident.

"So Louis and Anders went and got the shotgun," Cici continued as steadily as she could. "Tom kept it loaded in the corner of our living room in case of rattlesnakes," and here Cici grimaced at the irony. "Louis let Anders carry it. The safety wasn't on. As the three of them were walking toward the property's edge, Anders lifted the gun to see if it was loaded and it went off. The bullet ripped through Louis's groin area. When I heard the shot and the scream I went running in the direction, hoping that if a person had been hit it was Tom. But Tom was running toward me, carrying Louis whose blood was squirting like it was coming out of a hose. I almost fainted when I saw him, but I knew that I had to help him, help my son. I became strangely calm and took off my sarong, ripping it into bands to make a tourniquet, even though I had never used a tourniquet before."

"Oh my god, Cici," Julianne said, punctuating the momentary silence while Cici wiped at the tears that were streaming down her face and ran her sleeve against her nose to clear the snot away.

"Unfuckingbelievable," Cici whispered.

Julianne's own face was streaked with tears. She searched the park for sight of Alex, who was examining an injured dragonfly, running his finger along the translucent wings.

Cici continued. "Louis was losing blood so fast. We got the tourniquet on and put him in the back of the truck. I climbed in next to him, shading his face from the sun with my hands. Poor Anders had to sit in the cab with Tom. When we got to the hospital in Cottonwood, Louis had lost so much blood. I was covered in it."

Julianne wasn't sure why she thought that if she reached out and touched Cici, it would make her friend mad. She kept her hands pressed into her lap.

"The hospital in Cottonwood didn't have enough O negative blood to replace all Louis's lost blood, so they did their best to stop the bleeding and ordered a life flight to Phoenix. By the time we arrived at St. Joseph's, his blood oxygen levels were so low that he was in a coma. He stayed in the coma for three months, and the doctor's told us that if he woke up, he'd be a vegetable." Cici could barely control herself now. Her voice devolved into gasping sobs. "I was so depressed, I didn't even realize that Tom and I made a decision to pull the plug."

Horrified, Julianne threw her arms around her friend and pulled Cici toward her, letting her friend drench her shoulder with snot and tears. When Cici finally pulled away, the look on her face was pure desperation.

"He was almost an Eagle Scout," she said. "He had just earned a badge in fucking *Riflery*."

....

This year, Alex was old enough for kindergarten, although he would be the youngest in his class, so Julianne could, if she so desired, defer his enrolment for another year.

She was having him tested for Gifted and Talented. If he could get into the GT program, he would be guaranteed smaller class sizes, which would statistically diminish the amount of germs he came in contact with.

Whenever he started - this year or next - the sheer number of germs hovering inside and outside the walls (on the desks, the play equipment, the toilet seats, the other kids, especially the other kids) terrified Julianne. She fretted that germs would conquer Alex, worm their way through the cracks in his skin caused by his eczema and ravage him from the bones out. It was a medical fact that eczema increased the threat of serious skin infections, such Methicillin-Resistant Staphylococcus Aureus.

Julianne knew all about MRSA. She lived in terror of this particular germ because 1) it could eat up the body, causing unbearable pain while doing so, and 2) it was smarter than the smartest drugs that the smartest people could concoct. With Alex's eczema located primarily on his hands and wrists, Julianne feared that his every contact with a desk, monkey bar, or bare hand jeopardized his life.

As she threaded through traffic on her way to the interview she'd snagged with the counsellor of Foote Elementary, she checked on Alex in the rear-view mirror.

"Finger out of your nose," she scolded.

Alex lowered his head so that she couldn't see him.

"You know what lives on your fingers, underneath your fingernails?" she heard herself saying. One part of her urged her to not say another word, but a larger, fiercer part, like an alien invading her and holding her hostage, continued. "A million microscopic microbes are living solely to find a nose just like yours. These malicious things have been around for billions of years, and do you know why?"

Alex stared out the window at the gray sky, the dirty cars manoeuvring the construction pylons on Richmond.

"Because little boys and little girls like you can't keep their fingers out of their noses." The sound of her voice seared her brain in half. She nearly drove into one of the orange construction zone pylons set up to narrow the street from two lanes into one. Against her will it seemed, she kept on. "Inside your body, these germs cause a cold, diarrhoea, serious illness, death."

"Mommy, stop!" Alex howled.

"And you know what?" she continued. "You don't know which germs you get because they have figured out how to be invisible!"

"Mommy," Alex pleaded. "Don't say that."

Julianne took a hard right and pulled the car over, halting beside the curb on Mandell Street. She reached into her glove compartment feeling for the squirt bottle of antibacterial gel. Finding it, she noted it was nearly empty. She slapped the bottle cap against her hand then shot the remaining liquid into her palm. Turning around, she reached into the back seat.

"Here," she said, "Take this and rub it on your hands."

"No!" Alex said.

"Yes, Alex. If you're going to pick your nose, then I want your fingers to be clean."

"I'm not going to pick my nose anymore," he cried.

"You will. You do it all the time. You don't even know you're doing it."

"Nooooooooooooo!" Alex's scream pierced her right ear.

"Alex! When I tell you to do something, I expect you to do it."

"It stings," he whimpered.

"It won't sting for long," she said. She reached out and grabbed one of his hands, transferring the gel to his skin. He screamed in pain as the astringent penetrated the scrapes, bright red and raw from his scratching.

"Give me your other hand," she demanded.

"No, mommy. Please."

"Wipe that gel on your other hand," she demanded.

"No."

"Do it. We're going to sit here until you do."

Alex lost it then, screaming and crying and kicking the back of the driver's seat.

"I wish you didn't exist!" he yelled.

Instead of letting him have his tantrum, Julianne snapped. Opening her car door, she got out and yanked open the back door next to Alex's booster seat.

"You want me not to exist?!" she said. "Then get out of the car! You can stay here, and I'll leave. Then, I won't exist."

Alex gaped at her, his eyes wet with fat tears. "No," he choked. "No, mommy. Please don't leave me."

Julianne's knees gave way and she crumpled to the pavement, the heat from the rough asphalt bleeding through her pants. She felt as if she were about to split out of her own skin. Burying her face in her hands, she screamed into her palms and sobbed, hating herself to the brink of insanity. By that point, they had missed the GT interview. She heaved herself up and pushed the booster seat toward the middle of the back seat so that she could sit next to her son. He cringed when she touched his face, trying to comfort him.

"I'm so sorry, Alex." The ache inside her chest seemed to pulverize her bones.

As she drove home, she glanced often in the rear view mirror at her son. His face, its beauty, its vulnerability, the aliveness of him, pained her more than she could bear.

"I'm so sorry, baby," she repeated. "I would never leave you. I would never do that."

She barely kept her eyes on the road, trying to catch Alex's eye in the mirror. He wouldn't look at her. He rolled his head back and forth against the gray cloth seat.

"Alex?" she said. "Are you okay?"

He didn't answer her.

"I'm just trying to keep you safe, honey," she said.

"Stop, mommy," he said without meeting her gaze.

She decided not to tell Leo they'd missed the GT interview. She'd called to tell him, but when she heard his voice on the phone, gauged the mood he was in, she suspected he'd only be angry, so she lied when he'd asked how it went, told him the counsellor had cancelled it due to illness.

At home, Leo hovered uncomfortably close to her while she prepared dinner.

"So we've decided to send him to regular school?" Leo said

"We haven't decided anything yet, Leo," Julianne countered, feeling the fight well up inside her.

"Jules, he needs to go to school. You've said it yourself that it'll drive you insane if he stays home next year."

"I'm just worried that – "

"I know what you're worried about—"

"Is it my fault," she railed, "that he could go into anaphylactic shock? That he's got eczema? Asthma? I'm bringing it on him?"

Leo didn't say anything, and his silence infuriated Julianne. He went to the refrigerator and pulled out a Shiner. "Want one?" he asked, holding the beer out behind him.

She shook her head no.

Leo popped the cap off with the sharp side of a knife. "And you know what?" He resumed his post at the counter and took a long swig of beer.

He's going to say Alex needs a childhood, Julianne thought to herself.

"We've got to let the kid be a kid."

It pissed her off that he hadn't said something else, something she couldn't predict. "But he's not any kid, Leo, he's –"

"And I'm *sick* of your labelling him physically challenged! It isn't doing him any favours, Jules."

They were silent for a moment. Alex played with his plastic Noah's ark on the rug in the middle of the den.

"How did the mediation go?" Julianne asked to change the subject back to something she and Leo could talk about semi-neutrally.

Leo set the beer on the counter before him, removed his glasses and pinched the bridge of his nose. "Good," he said. "Doris is turning out –"

"Who's Doris?" Julianne interrupted.

"The new associate; she clerked with us this summer?" Leo answered.

Julianne's last bit of calm evaporated when Leo mentioned Doris. She imagined this Doris small and trim, dressed in slimming black pencil skirts that flattered her waxed calves, starched jewel toned shirts, form fitting black blazers, and two and a half inch Prada heels, a Fulbright and Jaworski Doris Day.

"She's working this trial with you?"

"Yes." He held out his beer, looking at Julianne with an expression that said, "and…?"

"Is she married?" Julianne asked.

"I don't know." Leo picked up his beer and guzzled a third of it.

"Well, is she wearing a ring?" Julianne asked. She knew that this line of questioning was moving them in the wrong direction, away from neutrality, but she couldn't help it. If they were in trial together, how could he not know?

"No ring. And anyway, it's irrelevant! Why are you changing the subject?" Leo said, his voice rising in pitch.

Julianne flipped a burger - too soon she noted because it was grey and sick looking, not nicely browned. She inhaled and exhaled slowly, attempting to keep her lips from pursing, her nose from wrinkling, her shoulders from hunching. Staring Leo down, she said, "You think it's my fault. I know you do."

"The kid can't fucking breathe, Jules."

Julianne hit each of the hamburgers with the spatula, pressing the biggest to see how much blood came out of it.

"And I *don't* say Alex is physically challenged," she continued. "I say 'special needs.'" She stretched her jaw open as wide as it would go, and stuck out her tongue, attempting to relax the tension in her face.

"What the hell are you doing?" Leo glared.

"A yoga posture for the face."

"Jesus Christ," Leo said.

"It's called the Lion!" she defended herself.

"You're insane," he mumbled.

Julianne flung the spatula toward him, accusingly. Bits of hamburger flung off the tip of it onto Leo's white starched shirt. "Don't!" she hissed. "Don't you *dare* insinuate I'm crazy."

"I am not *insinuating*." His tone was measured and clipped. He picked the meat globs from his shirt, flicking at the grease spots they left behind.

"I'm going to the dry cleaners tomorrow," she mumbled. She flipped the hamburgers again.

"Whatever," Leo said. He finished his beer, left the empty on the counter and went into the den. Alex lay on the floor, pushing the plastic Noah's ark around the rug.

Julianne strangled her urge to call her husband back to the kitchen area to finish their fight. Bubbling burger grease popped and spit up at her cheek.

She knew Alex had heard every word, the entire conversation, not only heard it but absorbed it - this conflict between her and Leo firing itself into their son's neural network: *this is what love looks like, sounds like, smells like, feels like*. Her heart broke even more for Alex than it already had that day. She smacked the burgers with the spatula and fretted about serving meat that had been agitated by her infuriated energy: *this is what love tastes like*.

Julianne watched Leo crouch down on his haunches in the living room next to their son.

"How's it going little man?" Leo asked.

Alex did not look up at his father. "Okay," he said.

She did not want to lose her husband; the thought of having to parent by herself petrified her. Instinctively, she starting praying the *Hail Mary*, a prayer she remembered from her Catholic school days.

> *Hail Mary, full of grace, the Lord is with thee...*

Leo stretched out, his back against the couch, and reached over to ruffle his son's hair. Alex vroomed the Noah's Ark.

"Play with me, daddy," he said.

> *Blessed art thou among women, and blessed is the fruit of thy womb...*

Tears welled in Julianne's eyes.

"You be the guy lion, okay?" Alex handed Leo a plastic lion.

Leo took the toy animal and bounced it around on the carpet. "Rooooar," Leo said. "Storrrrrm clouds are gatherrrrrring. Looks like a rrrrrrrager is heading our way."

Alex giggled and flung open the door to the toy ark. "Get in! I'll save you."

> *Holy Mary, Mother of God, pray for us sinners...*

Leo tromped the lion up the ramp and pushed it into the ark.

"Okay!" Alex said, "ready to go?"

> *Now, and at the hour of our death...*

"What about the lady lion?" Julianne called from the kitchen area.

Alex scrunched his brows but didn't look at his mother. "I don't know," he said. "I think she might be lost."

The Maclaren
by Marie Marshall

I've become fascinated by old monochrome film
from WW2 of the Spitfire – how its undercarriage
folds into its belly, and suddenly an ungainly crow
becomes the bonniest bird that ever flew.

The man who made that happen built this push-chair,
the buggy that folds at the push of a finger and tucks
into the corner by the front door, or slips onto
the bus's luggage rack as neat as a hasp into a staple,
so that I can pick you up and breathe in the baby-smell
on your head and sticky fingers and heft the folding miracle
with my free hand.

There's a slick art to hanging a plastic bag
from the handles, a balance to calculate so that you,
swinging your legs, slumped, open-mouthed at the world,
won't tip the whole ensemble backwards as I stop
by the last row of houses to look at the hills
(still streaked by snow, the radio mast tipped with
a little fire as the sky grows pale, late, slate-coloured).

When I look down at you and you look back,
I remember when they put you against my shoulder
and stood round to coo; I didn't recognize you
– monkey? gnome? walnut? something I failed
  to make milk for? –
now I find myself wanting to tuck you back in my belly,
and to become the sleek, roaring, flying machine I never was.
I pretend a coughing fit paints my face and makes it hot.

Yearning for Makeover: Jane Austen, Stacy and Clinton, and the Undaunted Nature of Writer's Block
by Angélique Jamail

I've read *Pride and Prejudice* several times and seen the movie – both the comprehensive A&E version and Joe Wright's brilliant 2005 release – several dozen times. Why do I love this story so dearly? There are many reasons, not the least of which is my fascination with the idea that people can change. They can change who they are, their foibles and character flaws, and become greater than they were through the quest of plot and character development. Perhaps this is why I love fiction so much; I am enamoured of Story.

The love story between Elizabeth Bennet and Fitzwilliam Darcy borders on the unfair. How could any mortal tryst live up to the extraordinary passion and chemistry that Keira Knightley and Matthew Macfadyen display onscreen? (I take gleeful encouragement from the fact that my husband of quite a long time delights in this movie possibly even more than I do.) The only thing more dynamic than these two characters' love for each other is their individual capacity for change as a result of the other's influence. The idea that one could be transformed, so shocked out of the comfortable surety of personal cynicism and into the loving embrace of exquisite romance and the humbling epiphany of the inner beauty of one's social nemesis – well, it gives me warm fuzzies. I love a good redemption story. I want to be Lizzie Bennet when I grow up.

....

When I was on maternity leave with my second child, my first child was about to turn two years old. I was exhausted from sleep-deprivation and the weary life-education of a toddler who, like most in her age group, personified the cutely vicious phrase "bundle of energy." I could remember what it was like to have energy, and I also knew that when I had it was a long time ago. I used to write things. Poems, stories, essays, even a libretto now and then. And in the previous year or so, I'd had the worst case of writer's block. I blamed this on many things, including my darling offspring. But I could not deny that at the heart of everything, I was a procrastinator, one who failed to cultivate a sturdy sense of discipline in my youth, one who was now hoping the holy grail of consistent routine would magically leap forth like Athena from my fatigued brain and save me. When you have very little free time in the first place, it's easy to let yourself not make time for things which take a lot of effort, such as actual self-improvement. You might ask what, during those months, I liked to fill those scant free, personal moments with, rather than writing. Fortunately, I have always enjoyed reading, very much, and I did this as often as I could. But sometimes I liked to "vegetate," though without abandoning the powers of contemplation, and in those moments you would find me in front of the television, watching either a DVD like *Pride and Prejudice* or TLC's *What Not to Wear.*

I'm not kidding. I loved that show. And unfortunately, watching it on television allowed me to *think* about changing myself but not actually do very much.

Like many people in our society, I am borderline-obsessed with makeover shows. HGTV feeds my design addiction, but WNTW (an acronym used by many of the postpartum mamas on a message board I frequented) nurtures that place inside of me where a woman who once thought herself stylish believes she can be so again. I don't think it's a coincidence that all those postpartum mamas adored this show. Having children and the appropriate ensuing devotion to them can severely compromise one's sense of self, though hopefully only temporarily. And let's be frank: there's no point in wearing nice clothes until your baby has learned not to spit up. This takes months. And by then, you may or may not have found a way to fit back into your old clothes anyway. The fantasy that Stacy London and Clinton Kelly will show up to surprise you with five large to spend on a new wardrobe is a powerful one.

Let's examine their process. *They* ambush *you*. This means you don't have to seek them out for help; they come to wherever you are, like the pizza delivery guy or angels of fashion mercy from kozmo.com. Then they take away all your old clothes. Yes, they make fun of them and probably of you in the process, but they deal with the literal mess of out-with-the-old so you don't have to, providing you with the clean sweep you were emotionally incapable of accomplishing but which you so desperately needed. (Just ask your friends and family who nominated you to be ambushed in the first place.) Stacy and Clinton give you rules to follow while you're out shopping for a new visual identity, so you don't have to figure it out by yourself, and when you flounder in the exhausting nightmare of boutique hell, they come in cavalry-style and save your ass. Then Nick and Carmindy come in and finish making you beautiful. You go home, debut your new and improved self for family and friends, and an international audience gets to watch as you end your week of cathartic soul-searching and wrenching transformation with the cheering of bouquet-bearing loved ones at the extraordinary and awe-inspiring butterfly you have become. Go, little caterpillar, *go*!

Abusers, criminals, terrorists, and other psychopaths aside, I think most people are basically good, and basically not completely miserable. But comparatively few "regular" people are really blissful; at least, they aren't blissful enough not to yearn for the fantasy of the makeover, at least from what I've seen. I suspect people love makeover shows so much because these shows give us faith; they help us to believe that change is possible. To quote a hundred zillion platitude-spouting Disney movies, dreams can come true. I may be generally happy with my life, but I kinda want to be Stacy London when I grow up.

....

I earned a degree in Creative Writing in the 1990s from a prominent university for this field of study. I ended up doing my thesis in poetry, although I'd started out as a fiction student. I enjoy reading a variety of genres – a broad palate, one might generously say. And I enjoy writing in any genre I like to read. This is not a stretch of logic.

However, because of said broad palate, you can expect me to write more than just literary fiction. At the time I was going to this particular school, an admission of such tastes was tantamount to heresy. So in order to feel comfortable enough to share my "non-literary," *genre* manuscripts with the world, I've had to overcome quite a lot of snobby conditioning that I was wasting my time because there was no serious market for anything other than literary fiction.

The fact that J.K Rowling made the billionaires list in 2007 - and was the first author ever to do so - is rather gratifying.

Her story has always inspired me: going from being a single mom on the dole with a tale scribbled on a ream of paper in a cardboard box but not enough money to buy her child more than a shoeboxful of toys, to being the author of one of the most successful literary franchises in history, is pretty tough to beat.

She inspired me, but not quite enough to put pen to paper and write my own damn novel – that had, I might add, been swimming around in my head for a rather long time. During my year of writer's block, I turned out maybe three new manuscripts, all of them quite brief, none of which were my novel. I didn't think I was just lazy, but that would be an easy and even comforting excuse. Laziness can be surmounted.

Can't it? God, I hope so.

....

"Well behaved women rarely make history." Surely by now most people have seen this expression emblazoned across spaghetti-strapped tank tops and bumper stickers. Truly, we - and I don't mean just women - have to make over the moulds society dictates for us if we want to impress any significant mark upon the world. After all, with so many billions of us on this planet, it's easy to get lost in the annals of the human condition. Hopefully we choose to cut our swathes across history in constructive ways.

But what about these characters I so admire? Not exactly the admittedly stereotypical embodiment of a grrrl, Stacy London wears high heels and make-up all the time, and I know that hairstyle takes longer than five minutes every morning. (But then I guess even Ani diFranco puts her appearance together before she steps onstage.) Lizzie Bennet has to give up her stubborn streak to get the man and the happy ending. She has to give up her pursuit of making Darcy her own personal victim for snubbing her - in other words, to sacrifice what she believes or thinks she wants. In some respects, so do Elinor and Marianne Dashwood from *Sense and Sensibility* and Emma from the novel which bears her name. They each must let go their idealistic patterns or pursuits in order to earn their happiness. Happiness which ultimately, after all, takes the form of a man. They must become - and fill in your personal favourite: demure, accepting, humble, apologetic - to get their bliss. And then, as in a Shakespearean comedy or a fairy tale, their stories end in marriage.

How do we reconcile this with the common impression that Jane Austen's heroines are so ahead of their time? We take from Austen's own unmarried life that she chose not to yoke herself unto a man but instead published under her own name and made quite a mark critiquing her society through the entertaining vehicle of the novel. Kudos to her, but I wonder what she really wanted for herself, and whether she ultimately earned it or had the opportunity to enjoy the fruits of such earnings.

....

I have heard that babies – those perpetual changers and harbingers of change themselves - who are born with navy blue eyes (as both my children were), whose eyes become lighter blue in their first few months, will end up with a different eye colour. The eyes of babies born with lighter blue irises will likely not change. I spent a lot of time gazing into my infant son's sapphire orbs and wondering what colour they would end up being: gray-green like his father's or hazel like his sister's and mine? I don't even know how many hours I lost just staring at his sleeping, breathing form. So many women lose themselves in the flush of new parenthood. They abandon every hobby and pastime for the extraordinary, joyful challenges of being a mother. *Good for them!* we say. *They have the right idea! You* should *give over yourself in order to give of yourself. How else can you be a good mother without being devoted entirely to your new and dependent creature?*

Yes, of course. To some extent, I agree. But how can I consciously allow myself to be lost? I don't mean worrying about what happened to my cute, pre-pregnancy body (though I certainly did that, too). How dare I deprive my children of a mother who is a full person? How can I give my daughter an appropriate role model if I have sacrificed my identity? When am I going to get back to doing the things that made me an interesting person before I was a mom? Will I still get my own personal, not-lived-vicariously-through-my-children happiness, or am I trying to have my cake and eat it, too?

I had often wondered whether I really enjoyed being a writer as much as I enjoyed *the idea* of being a writer. Yes, *the idea* is intoxicating. But I also really do love the writing process - drafting and especially revision - and so writer's block is particularly painful. In conversation with a colleague, I once compared my writing ability to a large cookie. (I was pregnant, we were eating lunch, food was always on my mind.) And I told her that I felt like each passing season in which I didn't publish something took a bite out of that cookie, and I anxiously believed myself in danger of its being imminently consumed. After a year of writer's block, I was afraid. And here I was about to have another baby - not exactly a way to create more free time.

So what did I do? I signed up for an advanced fiction workshop with a teacher I admired and gave myself some serious, imminent deadlines. Deadlines to produce new manuscripts, good manuscripts, with the intention of defibrillating my writing career while not making an idiot of myself in front of some very accomplished writers and editors. *If I'm ever going to do this,* I told myself, *it's going to be now.* I sat in that group and thought really hard about the story that had been percolating inside my head for a while, bumping around awkwardly like Athena with her shield and spear trying not to hurt me. I put a chapter on paper, then a second and a third, and submitted them for workshop. The pages were taken seriously. Then the workshop ended.

And then, I did it. I wrote the novel. It's done.

I wrote a novel? How surreal.

I wouldn't mind being J.K. Rowling when I grow up, and I'm already so far past thirty it's almost not worth mentioning.

I guess I'd better get going.

Mother & Son
by Valerie Walawender

Imperial Signet
by Judith Field

Judith, 2013

Behind the old 78 records that we don't have the technology to play, hides an Imperial Signet. A portable typewriter I inherited from my mother, the writer. She bought it in the late nineteen sixties, in the days when motherhood meant staying at home. And if you wanted to work, the job ads in the paper were divided into Men's Jobs and Women's Jobs.

There's a stash of magazines in which her stories appeared, containing articles about cooking and knitting, or the pill and abortion, depending on the target age group. It was fine to read about it, and write about it, but God help you if you were caught living the permissive life. There was a real dual standard and men expected to marry a virgin. Every magazine's problem page seemed to include at least one referral to the National Council for the Unmarried Mother And Her Child (the organization we now know as Gingerbread).

One of my mother's earliest stories, called "All I've got", is about just such an unmarried mother. The character, a single violinist, has given birth and is recovering in a home where the babies are put up for adoption. Her own mother, a single parent, is adamant that she should give the baby up so that her musical career will not be hampered. The baby's father is on the scene but seems to have had no say in the matter and it appears to be assumed that the she will give the baby up. But she changes her mind.

The typewriter is the sort of thing I don't suppose many of us have seen for a long time. Smelling of the grey metal of which it is made, about the size of the laptop I use every day. There are keys with weird symbols of which I've forgotten the meaning. I try them. One seems to do nothing till I remember it's the margin release – giving the typist authorial freedom to go past the margin (which you set with a little sliding thing), right off the end of the page if I don't pay attention.

It also has a key that will type a decimal point. Not much use to a fiction writer, and then just as now, there is no single key I can hit that will fill a page with deathless prose. Must use that in one of my works of speculative fiction. I'll put it in my ideas bank, a pretentious name for a word document. But I'd better come up with a less clichéd description than "deathless prose".

I put in a piece of paper, type a few words as a reminder of what the output looks like; it's a long time since anyone used it. I hit a key (and hit is the right word – it's hard work) and a metal lever comes out and strikes the ribbon, imprinting the letters onto the page. I can't change the basic 12 point Courier font or its size, and there's no delete or erase facility.

What a din it makes when I use it, "hammering" we called it, when my mother was typing her stories and novels. The last stage after longhand drafting, redrafting, reading to the teenage me:

"What shall I call the boyfriend in this one?"

"Tony."

"No, don't like that. Steve."

"Again?"

Double spaced, big margins, carbon paper sandwich. She had a wooden desk in the back bedroom we called the "writing room", my father's metal writing desk was in the opposite corner. For some reason it was the only room they hadn't put a radiator in, they'd kept the gas fire. Blue faded lino on the floor. Two authors in a Liverpool garret.

We kids got the carbon copies for drawing paper. Were we scribbling on the back of untold and unsold tales? Perhaps so, I have carbon copies of the ones that were published, a bag full of women's magazines, books on the shelves.

We didn't dare ask our parents about publication, didn't want to remind them that they were waiting – in those pre-email days of the nineteen sixties - for a letter fluttering through the door from the agent, or the knock of the postman with a manuscript too big for the letterbox. Name after name after name, from the Writers and Artists.

Locked in the typewriter's write-only memory, etched into its levers and springs, roller and ribbon, are forty stories, three novels, one woman's dream. Published. Deathless. Cut short at the age of 44.

....

Ruth, 1970

I started writing when my mother died, to fill up the days. I told people it was because now I could, once Peter started at school. *Ay* school – cross it out. I wish someone would invent a machine that corrected mistakes automatically. Only in science fiction. Judith loves that stuff, I can't see the appeal.

I don't know how some authors write straight onto a typewriter. I have to do it longhand, I can't type it out till I've finished. And even then, I make changes.

Matthew uses a great heavy Remington machine but I got this little one, the day I bought The Beatles "Revolver" album. Maybe I'll get an electric one if I sell more, they're easier on the wrist muscles (do they have muscles? Must ask Matthew).

I got a cheque for £20 for translation rights today. That Danish magazine *Hendes Verden* again, and a new Australian one. Not much "translation" needed there, all they did was change the phrase "good old British food" to "good old Australian food" and pounds to dollars.

Judith and Peter act like the fact that I write is just what we do in our house, they don't seem that interested, don't talk about it much. I asked Judith what she thought a "cigarette that looked like it had bled to death" would be, she said it'd be pale and white. Hmm...I meant covered in red lipstick stains. I'll put that in the novel anyway[1].

Rosemary is very good at placing my stories. She knows what sells. First it was cosy stories, then they all had to have sad endings. Then they had to have mild sex scenes, now the latest thing the mags want is two endings, for the reader to choose which they prefer. Next time I go to London to sit and drink *Punt e Mes* with her during our Quaglino lunch, I'll ask about the novel – what do the publishers say?

She thinks this is my first but it's actually my third – the other two toe-curlers lie exhausted inside a cardboard folder, in a plastic bag, in the back of the wardrobe behind the dinner jacket, cocktail dresses, fur coat and Matthew's rifle. When the police come round to check the firearms certificate all they do is sit and drink whisky *all evening*, we may as well hang the guns on the living room wall and line up the bullets on the mantelpiece for all they care. Must put that into a story[2].

---

[1] She did

[2] She didn't, but perhaps I will.

Sprinting With a Leg Cramp
by Jennifer James

"Mommy can I watch *Yo Gabba Gabba*?"
The sweet, high pitched voice of my daughter intrudes juuust as I've begun to achieve terminal velocity on my work in progress. The pink, cherubic cheeks, large blue eyes, and fine, wispy blonde baby curls that frame her face are the camouflage employed by Mother Nature to keep me from eating my own young. She pats my leg, a drum roll that starts at half beats, increases to quarters, and then rolls right on into a sixteenth running out of her tiny, chubby fingers.

It's like this every time. I sit down, begin to write, and in minutes my daughter is screaming at me to do something for her. She ignores me most of the time, breaking out her uncanny ability to interrupt my writing the very moment I seem to have found my groove. The sweet spot where words flow without conscious thought and plots spin themselves without effort.

She's persistent, vocal, and understands that while I write, she can watch all the TV she wants. So I'm raising an intelligent, bossy kid. Great. The future student council president has claimed my living room as her personal dance/art studio and lunch room. Cracker crumbs nest in the couch cushion folds. Stains marr the flat surfaces of what is supposed to be durable, washable, miracle Micro-fibre, so easy to clean it'll induce spontaneous orgasms in mothers of young children coated in food, armed with markers and dripping, "leak proof" sippy cups. Three weeks after we bought our furniture, a cheap set meant to get us through the early years of kids, low income, and a general attitude of suburban survival in the great race of "we're not competing with what our neighbours have, but really we secretly are" my older child decided to write on a bunch of Post-It notes with a thick black Sharpie marker.

It bled through and left my couch with a spotty, discordant tattoo. Sharpie doesn't come out of fabric.

At least one product out there is true to its advertising.

"Mommy! I want to watch Yo. Gabba. Gabbaaaa!"

Yeah, well I want to stab DJ Lance Rock in the face with a fork. I swear this kid's show is written and produced by drug addicts. The whole thing is bizarre and strange and my kid can't get enough. The whole "Don't bite your friends" thing did come in handy though. What I can't teach my kid, twenty two minutes of trippy blaring kids programming can.

"MOMMY! I WANT YO GABBA GABBA!"

I know that I should tell her that she can't watch any more TV when she yells at me like this. And I generally do tell her that. But I'm also just as likely to let her have her way. Time to write is almost non-existent in my life, and so I find myself hitting the buttons on the Netflix queue and walking away…just in time for her to come after me with a sippy cup and ask for milk.

In fifteen minutes we'll go through the whole thing all over again. Fifteen beautiful minutes full of blaring, high pitched kid's music and cavorting characters in which I attempt to write in a sprint. My daughter dances in front of her babysitter and I swallow the guilt rising to the surface. My child is safe, fed, clean, and healthy.

And yet I'm taking time away from spending time with her to pursue my own goals. Something inside me says it's the wrong thing to do. Being a wife and mother means my life belongs to my husband and children first, to me second.

"I want the special pink bow right here."

How a tom boy who lives in ratty sneakers and jeans managed to birth a girly-girl is lost to me. When I was little I spent all my time chasing after and idolizing my older brother. I can catch a garden snake, painted turtle, or salamander with the best of them. Dirty nails and twigs in my hair were the norm. I rode my bike over plywood ramps, crashed mopeds, and lived in high top sneakers.

My oldest has somehow created her own persona, and I'm glad she has. I don't want tiny carbon copies running around without independent thoughts or dreams. She loves all things pink and sparkly.

But that doesn't mean I understand it.

I wore a flower hairpiece to a wedding this summer because she told me it was pretty. That's right; I take fashion advice from a six year old. She's got better taste in these things than I do. I'm much more at home playing in mud or riding my bike off curbs than I am in a dress.

She sometimes comes into my office and steals paper from the printer tray to staple together into packets that she illustrates and writes stories in. Most of her books revolve around convoluted and cannibalized Disney princess movies. Which is fine, except for the themes in most of those movies that revolves around needing a man to save you. So I often hop in and help with story development. Her princesses save themselves, and often their prince too. I'm a bit of a heavy handed editor, but I look at it as helping her develop a voice that doesn't follow the crowd of boy obsessed lemmings off a cliff on the belief a man is waiting at the bottom to catch her and cart her off into his five bedroom, three bath Mc Mansion.

I worry about that often, that my children will not be independent and able to care for themselves. They are bombarded with media messages telling them how to look, act, who to marry, and that a powerful male figure will swoop in and rescue them from their problems. The last thing I want is for my daughters to grow up subservient to and dependent on someone else. It's probably my biggest fear for them. Actually, no. Scratch that. Sexual abuse, kidnapping, murder, spousal abuse. So being dependent is number five, but in a way it ties into the first four.

Parenting is hard, muddled, and full of hidden chuck holes.

My mind races in circles often, worry that my taking time to write while they watch videos or play with toys that exemplify the very things I don't want for them is hurting them has worn a rut into my frontal cortex. If I am an example of a woman who has chosen to pursue a career that is more dream than reality at this point—a small business venture if you boil it down to numbers and models—am I doing a good job? I have no real income to speak of at this point from it. Writing for publication and the marketing efforts that go with it consume hours and entire days of my time in which I am not interacting with my children. Or my husband.

And a tiny part of me is ashamed to admit that I love it.

I love being alone.

I love working on something that is just for me. Without distractions, tiny hands on my legs, cries for food or drink or clean laundry.

I'm supposed to be a care giver. The cog in the household that keeps things running in a smooth manner. As a woman, that's the traditional, hetero-normative role I am to assume. The great mantle of social responsibility that's going to transform America!

I pretty much suck at it in any traditional sense. I love my family. My husband, kids, the dog and cat. But I also love pursuing my own interests and at times feel this huge well of resentment bubbling beneath the surface, molten, thick, and ready to spew forth. Why should I have to drop what I'm doing for everyone else? Why should I put my needs and career aspirations on the back burner in favor of everyone else?

And yet. Yet. The guilt and the shame that consume me when I feel that I've failed as the caregiver and nurturer threaten to swallow me whole and drown me in my aspirations.

"You're always on the computer."

This is the crux of having an office at home. I try to split my time between my family, my school work, and my writing. I quit my job when my mother had a heart attack.

Everyone told me the lie: "You'll have so much more time to write now."

Ha. Fuckers.

Now that I'm home more, my family expects more of me. More cleaning, more cooking, more nurturing. The independent children I thought I was raising are becoming increasingly needy and unwilling to care for themselves.

Any time I try to sneak away to my upstairs office is suspect. I bring my laptop down to the dining room table and attempt to work there but it's futile. If I'm on the computer I'm not paying attention to them. My older girl is particularly sensitive to this. I suspect it is partially due to the fact that I worked outside the home for so much of her life, and now her sibling gets alone time with Mommy. Sibling rivalry is so awesome.

The minute my computer appears, it's time to interrupt Mommy.

"Are you famous?"

No one ever told me that writing genre fiction required so much marketing. Part of marketing: giving away swag. Promo keepsakes for readers. I autograph endless piles of cardboard with my book cover and blurb on them while my kids play. I worry that they'll get the paint markers I'm using and write all over the walls or something with them so while I scrawl my pseudonym I plot places I can hide the markers, and hide the text of the blurb as much as possible. I admit I failed when I didn't consider that my oldest would be reading so well, so quickly.

And what does she want to read? Whatever I'm working on. As an erotic romance author, my sex scenes are plentiful and graphic. I'm not ready to have a discussion with my child about the meaning of the three "C" words. The minimize button and I are so tight, we have a weekly poker night.

My career (if you can call it that) is in its infancy. Of course, the best way to increase sales is to keep writing new books. But I've also got to spend precious hours mailing, autographing, and promoting on the internet…while watching the kids. Most days I get very little actual writing done. I'm too busy thwarting tiny fingers from smudging ink or finding the right episode of Blue's Clues or making peanut butter and jelly sandwiches. No crusts.

"Are you going to be up there all day or what?"

My husband is rarely home. He works overtime, all the time. It's selfish and wrong of me, but when he is home I try to foist the children off on him so that I can sneak in some uninterrupted writing time.

It sounds like a good plan.

Except that it never really works out.

He loiters in the doorway of my office or in the chair in the corner asking me questions about anything. Everything. He's interested in my day, my life, in me. It's wonderful and irritating all at once. I love him. I want to spend time with him. And I also have this really great story idea loitering at the horizon line, and if I get ten minutes alone it might coalesce into my break out book. The book that finally pushes me from obscurity into the ranks on Amazon. We chit chat, and the amorphous smoke of plot and conflict and inspiration shreds before I can jot it down. It's maddening, and my husband ends up bearing the brunt of my irritation.

Like most couples we've gone through periods of absolute bliss and months of borderline hatred. But we keep forging ahead, and both of us try to be attentive to the other. Sometimes it's an epic fail.

The children run in and out of the room poking me to get them food or drinks or toys. I look pointedly at him and he leaves…but not before I end up feeling like a schmuck.

I should be spending time with him, but I have deadlines.

And I'm selfish enough to want uninterrupted writing time.

It never works out for long, but I want it.

We try to institute blocks of time in the schedule dedicated to my business. The business of being Jennifer James. So far it's hit and miss.

Every time I have to get up from my desk to pour juice or make a sandwich, the coals I'd been banking to ignite a true writing sprint is lost and scattered.

Doused in a splash of river water and utterly useless.

So I begin anew, and hope I can find my sweet spot before the dog wants to go outside to poop.

"How much longer?"

I hear this question so often. It has many connotations, and I hate them all.

How much longer will I write? I can't not write. But I've tried. I tried to bury it, stomp it out of existence. But voices clamour in my head, compete with those of my family, all of them want attention and they want it now. The more I deny them, the angrier they get. Discordant notes hit ear splitting heights. I fall into a pit of depression.

To not write is to deny my true self. My life gushes from my fingertips in sprints and trickles. I try to balance on a thin flexible rope suspended above a pit riddled with unmet expectations and broken promises. Love for my family overcorrects me to the left, love of self to the right. The heavy weight of societal expectations is a rock laden chain draped around my waist and tangling my feet.

And I inch forward. Everyday. Sometimes I fall down.

But I still hope that one day, I can soar. That I can rise off the rope and achieve some kind of Zen balance where I'm not in a constant war with myself.

Everyone wants to know how much longer.

You'll have to ask the clock maker how many times he wound my springs.

Interview with Professor Alison Bartlett
May 2013

by Kasia James

Our reality is a fragile thing, made up largely in our own minds. The complexity of this goes far past the simple 'glass half-full (or empty)' lens of mood, and is interwoven by all the stories we encounter in our lives, both good and bad. This is especially true in the arena of motherhood, where well meaning advice from friends and relatives blend with the more polished messages in marketing, and the insinuations of pseudo-science. Stories are powerful in changing the way we view our experiences, and the choices we make about ourselves and our children. Words can entangle you, or free you.

Alison Bartlett is, by profession at least, a woman of words. As Chair of Women's Studies at the University of Western Australia, she has published extensively, especially on the subject of breastfeeding and women's literature. In person, she is highly articulate and chooses her words carefully, but thankfully is light-hearted and irreverent.

Language is evidently a subject close to her heart, and one which she feels shapes our experience and expectations of motherhood. The words that we take on from outside sources, and those that we use ourselves. Discussing the external information available to women, she says, "There are all these books which come out every year, which just seem to profess the same sorts of things about what to expect. They just seem really confined in their sets of terminology and topics."

Information from books, or the lack of it, was one of the motivating factors to get Alison interested in the field in which she works. She says, "I had my daughter, and I started reading all these books, going: 'Oh God! Where are all the feminist books on this?' In my study I'd been doing all this feminist theory about bodies, and when I came to have a baby, all the stuff I could find was from the seventies. There didn't seem to be anything in the nineties. That's how I started investigating."

Magazines these days are no better. "I think there are limited ways in which we can talk about it," Alison suggests. "The women's magazines and pregnancy magazines have one way of talking about motherhood which is evident in the limited kinds of words they use all the time. In order to resist those stories and narratives of what you're meant to do in your life, you need to invent your own way of discussing the issues. Part of that is purely linguistic."

She recognizes, however, that the sheer volume of material out there can be a barrier to women being able to think clearly about the issues of motherhood, especially when mothers have been targeted as a marketing niche. "It's hard work processing it all - making sense of it. Developing your own critical perspective, when it bombards you with all those commercial interests, constantly."

However, it seems like there is a huge opportunity now for women to start to develop their own stories, and express the real range of their experience. Alison says that for a few years after she gave birth, she collected poetry about the experience. "Poetry offers a really different way of talking," she says, "Because it's so crystalline in the way that it uses language and shapes imagery and stories in a small form."

Why hasn't this knowledge been documented before? "I guess you could say that women are too busy! Childbirth, for example, is difficult to articulate in its intensity. It's hard to describe, partly because we have no tradition or legacy of stories about it. I consciously made time to sit down and write about my birth so that I didn't forget, because I could feel it fading."

Alison also suggests that although there has been a lot written about other heroic events, such as war, they have been written about issues that traditionally involve men.

Women's stories haven't been part of our literary tradition in the West because their lives haven't been seen as worthy of literary merit.

The discussion may start to change in the West as the demographic of women becoming mothers starts to change. "Women are waiting until they're older to have babies, and often have done education post high-school, and have done some work in careers, and so are women of the world. It's not like they've gone from home to making their own home. So I think that shift hasn't been caught up with in terms of cultural expectations and literature available. Women start to become aware of it when they do give birth, and start to feel like they're back in a 1950's movie or something!"

Alison has started to see other, perhaps more worrying trends emerging too. "It could be a conspiracy theory," she laughs, "But people I see now who are pregnant - there is a greater range of foods which are forbidden because of the potential danger. It seems to increase all the time. Part of me is tempted to wonder whether it is a co-incidence: this increased surveillance of potentially maternal bodies, and the increased burden of being a 'proper mother' comes when women are at their greatest proportion of the workforce? There still seems to be some anxiety around women being professionals, and imagining women having careers throughout their adult life, not just until they have children."

Whether or not women are valued in the workplace for the skills they acquire as a mother is a moot point. "It's probably quite varied, depending on where you work," Alison muses. "My tendency would be to say that other mothers would be more cognisant of your circumstances and your increased capacities. I think that women who work and have families have increased life skills. At the same time, it's difficult making those kinds of suggestions about other mothers because women are often set up to compete with each other, rather than to collaborate. It's a really ingrained thread in social relations as well."

Sadly, even now when feminism has become so mainstream, much of the perceived value of a woman is still based on the way she looks, and of course much of the competition between women in society is set up around appearance. "So much depends still on whether you look like a motherly figure, or if you look like a worker! You can't tell from how someone looks, how they work, but there are so many assumptions based on appearance, much more intensively for women than for men. There is no such thing as looking 'fatherly'!"

"When men enter this domain of child raising, it's a whole new thing. I think there's an element of novelty to stay-at-home dads, where people aren't quite sure what to make of them. But also because he has discarded the privileges that go with masculinity in western capitalism, women recognize this as something to be admired."

It's a factor which she thinks is related to the intense political debate in recent years in Australia around Paid Parental Leave. "I've heard many arguments that Parenting Leave will never be fully accepted until senior men begin taking it and so making it normal for everyone to take time out from work in order to raise little human beings. When men start to value and aspire to the work women have done for hundreds of years, this also starts the work of unlinking particular values that are 'naturally' attributed to women (like the capacity to care and nurture) and which lock us into particular social positions, expectations and jobs. If men can care for babies, and women can be prime ministers, then perhaps people's capacities are not linked to gender."

Australia's first female Prime Minister, Julia Gillard, came in for a range of vicious criticism which seemed to centre to some extent on her gender, and which would not have been tolerated if the attacks were about race. One of the issues raised highlights a disjunction in the way that motherhood has been viewed historically. Ms Gillard was criticised for being 'deliberately barren' of all things, as if a women could only have value if she has children. However, the alternative role of being 'Just a Mum' also seems to lack intrinsic value. Alison thinks that this conflict - of both highly valuing and yet lacking respect for mothers - may have very deep roots.

"I reckon it's because of its attachment to the religious aspect. In Christianity, anyway, the Virgin Mary is practically the only female figure, besides Mary Magdalene who's more marginalised. There's a lot of complex and political history around her idealisation as a mother, and as a virgin mother, which makes it really complicated. That's been used by the Church and the State in different ways over time, and we're left with that lag, even though we're supposedly a more secular society. There's a hangover of motherhood being 'sacred' and yet because of - I'd call it patriarchal privilege [laughs]- it's not valued in practice."

One of the few positive role models we have been offered as mothers by the mass media in the last few years is that of the 'Yummy Mummy.' It's something which taps into the aspirational nature of celebrity watching, but also is another source of pressure on new mothers. Alison suggests that the 'Yummy Mummy' phenomenon is almost about hiding your role as a mother. "Really it's about looking as good as you did before you were a mother. You can efface the whole experience. Perhaps it states the obvious about how it is objectifying, and you can look as if you're not a mum, but sometimes these obvious things need stating."

Related to the issue of whether society values women, is whether we value ourselves. Part of that is being able to be 'selfish' to maintain a separate identity from our children. The loss of identity is something that many new mothers feel: that you even lose your own name and interests to become 'John's Mum' or 'Jane's mother', wholly branded by your progeny.

"When I recognised that, it clicked for me why earlier generations of hippies and alternative people got their kids to call them by their name. Every time you're called by your name, it's an affirmation of who you are. You're not just 'Mum' - that's just what you do!"

"I think it's really important to sustain those parts of your identity which are nurturing for you. That aphorism they say: "Happy Mum means a happy baby" is really true. You can easily let yourself be subsumed into your child's needs, but I don't think it's good for anyone."

"It's a pity that the word 'selfish' has such a negative meaning!" Alison laughs."As if you're not allowed to take notice of yourself. It's one of those discourses related to motherhood being sacrificial. It may be related to the Christian virtue of the sacrificing mother? I don't think it's good for women to continually sacrifice themselves to others' needs."

That said, how women think about their role, and the words they use to describe what they do becomes very relevant on this subject. Alison stresses that: "It's important not to feel it as a sacrifice. You look after babies because you want to - because you wouldn't want to do it any other way. Doing it in the name of love rather than sacrifice is a much more motivating factor for me!"

Breastfeeding is one the subjects which has been a real passion in Alison's career, although her focus is starting to move on now to object biographies - the way that certain objects are connected to the activism of a particular time and society. However, the giving of milk is one of the ways in which motherhood can be seen to be completely physically sacrificial for women.

"There can be resentment you feel when it's not reciprocal in benefit. You're giving of yourself to this other person, but you're not getting anything back. You can feel animalistic, rather than human, like a cow being milked at a factory. It's again one of the times when language is important. If you can find a different way to express a concept, you can reconceptualise it. If it's something that you want to do, something you get pleasure from doing, then it feels different."

"I'm not a 'You must breastfeed!' advocate," Alison explains, "Although I think it's a fantastic thing to do for a number of reasons, not just related to the baby's health. That really strong pressure you get to breastfeed is not as efficient as many medical professionals believe in encouraging women to breastfeed. I've been trying to open up the discussion and stories so that it becomes more 'woman-centred': so that women's experience becomes central to how it's perceived in the professional domain.

"Rather than saying: 'You must breastfeed your baby because breastfed babies have higher IQ,' or coming out with statistics to load on the guilt, I think there needs to be much more focus on the benefits for the Mum! It can be really pleasurable, and it's time out sitting down, and you can read, or watch TV, or look at your baby, or write poetry. There's also all sorts of fantastic hormones when you let down! I think there needs to be a much larger array of ways that you can talk about breastfeeding than the purely scientific way."

The pressure that women can feel to breastfeed is perhaps only the start of a much more sustained societal pressure to mother in a particular way. Alison recalls reading a book by Joan B. Wolf which made a great impression on her. "She makes this fantastic argument which makes so much sense to me about how mothering has become much more intensive in the last decade or two. It discusses how there is all this extra pressure, especially on educated, professional women to achieve higher outcomes."

"Having your baby close to you all the time, and spending lots of time developing them before preschool, because they're at formative stages. And then the pressure to make homemade things and cook homemade organic food. You're eating your own vegetables...it all piles on more and more expectations and more and more work, which always seems to be the mother's job. She calls it 'Intensive Mothering'. "

When talking about her own upbringing, Alison laughs when she recalls the lack of 'intensive mothering.'. "How did my Mum do it? She just didn't seem to be perturbed. I just remember her doing her own thing a lot of the time, and ignoring us! Just going to the shop when you need to, and buying cans...she wouldn't dream of having a vegetable garden of her own. They were just much more practical."

Intense mothering, that desire to be not only a perfect parent, but also to have a successful career and relationships, all takes time. Often lack of time is what can really lead to resentment in mothers. Alison herself found this to be an issue when she became a mother. "It really nagged at me for a long time, " she explains. "I always felt like I was short for time. Racing between work and home. We need to put it in a different perspective. Our idea of time is so industrial, so outcome centred. What can I get done in this time? Whereas, I think there are other conceptions of time, that are more conducive to breastfeeding! You've just got to give up on that factory time - that time is limited, and that you have to be productive, and that it's linear and going to run out. You've got to expand your sense of time, so that the moment becomes bigger, and more important. It's another way that language, and the way we talk about time, can change our experience of it."

Whether breastfeeding, trying to juggle mothering with work, or to fit in some time to fulfil your personal aspirations, the words we use to express those experiences can deeply affect our experiences of them. That alone makes it all the more important to have more than one, stereotypical and market driven perspective on being a parent.

"We have all these voices in our heads anyway, from parents and friends, partners and teachers, television and books, and they're always there. We decide which ones we prefer, but those ones we don't prefer just stick in there anyway! Part of the work of re-thinking it is expanding those stories, so that there are more of them, and there are more possibilities made available, to counter all the stories we don't want to hear."

In the end, Alison Bartlett is giving her account of being a woman and mother, and hoping that others will be to be able to tell their own stories. By doing so, they may construct their own realities. It's a confusing maze of information and misinformation, but as she says, "The best you can do, is the best you can do! We're always negotiating all of those discourses, expectations and pressures. There is an intense pressure on women to perform maternity to that really high aspirational degree, which makes it really difficult to remember to value yourself and the things that you love doing. It's an on-going conversation and negotiation you absolutely have to do, or you risk losing yourself."

Reasons to Breastfeed
by Alison Bartlett

Because it seriously disrupts the neoliberal autonomous unified western subject
Because I can still be a neoliberal autonomous unified western subject if I want
Because it feels good
Because it hurts
Because it transforms our understanding of breasts
Because it objectifies our breasts
Because my breasts lead the way
Because my breasts have never been so huge
Because it's sacred
Because it's sexy
Because leaky bodies are radical
Because it's easy to disguise any unwanted leaks
Because I like offending people in public
Because it's a private thing
Because it's political to do it in public
Because I can do it whenever I need to
Because it's convenient
Because it's inconvenient
Because it's cheap
Because it's anti-capitalist
Because it's anarchic
Because it's ordinary
Because it's miraculous
Because it's heroic
Bècause I'm a martyr
Because I don't care
Because it's easy
Because it's hard
Because it's hard to stop
Because I can stop if I want to
Because I don't want to stop

Because I like it
Because I like all the hormones
Because it's like being on drugs
Because it's an alternative state
Because it's spiritual, a Zen meditation
Because it gives me 15 minutes to put my feet up and stop work
Because it gives me 3 hours 4 times a day to put my feet up
Because I can watch TV when I'm doing it
Because I can read philosophy when I'm doing it
Because my body knows how to do it
Because my body doesn't know how to do it
Because my baby knows how to do it
Because it's a secret between us
Because everyone knows about it
Because my boyfriend doesn't want me to
Because my boyfriend wants me to
Because the midwife wants me to
Because I thought you had to
Because it's public health policy
Because my sister did
Because my mum didn't
Because I've got gallons of milk
Because I've hardly got any milk
Because I wouldn't know how much milk I've got and
Because it doesn't matter
Because I can't do it, and that's why I want to.

'Reasons to Breastfeed' was first published in Hecate vol 29 number 2, 2003.

A Century of Advice to Australian Mothers
by Dr. Carla Pascoe

I became a mother in January 2013. Like so many new parents, I turned to books and websites for advice on which side of the nappy was the front and why on earth babies aren't born knowing how to get themselves to sleep. Reading some of our contemporary instruction manuals for mothers and fathers, I began to wonder how much the science and folklore of 'mothercraft' has changed over time. As an historian, I cannot help but bring my professional training to bear on my mothering. Some family members have laughed that I approach my maternal role like a very important research project; surveying all the available literature and weighing up various arguments against each other. But the useful thing that my historian's mind has contributed to my mothering is that I am naturally sceptical of the confident tone of the 'expert'. We historians are all too aware that today's unquestionable truths will be queried and even mocked by the next generation!

What follows is a survey of advice given to mothers over the past century. Sometimes that advice seems hopelessly out-dated and quaint. At other times it appears surprisingly progressive and modern to our twenty-first century eyes. But what all these extracts from child-rearing manuals share is a strong sense of the solemnity and profundity of a mother's role. It is a weighty burden mothers carry when they are warned that their child's future happiness depends upon every tiny parenting decision the mother makes.

....

Parental Commandments: Or, Warnings to Parents on the Physical, Intellectual, and Moral Training of Children **(E. W. Cole: Melbourne, 1890)**

This child-rearing book was originally published in London and reissued in Melbourne, in an age in which anything coming from 'the mother country' was assumed to be more authoritative than books originating in the colonies. In late nineteenth century Australia, parental advice manuals were read by earnest mothers from the middle or upper classes: this book would have been very unlikely to find its way into working class hands. In 1890 Marvellous Melbourne was a booming city at its economic peak, blissfully unaware that it was about to be plunged into the severe depression of the 1890s. Here the anonymous author structures their dictates as a series of grim Victorian prohibitions: don't do this and don't do that.

Train your child and you train yourself; a new field is opened up, at once the most interesting, stimulating, instructive, and natural. The widest capacity and experience will here find ample scope, and the narrowest and smallest can be exercised and strengthened. Let us remember that every thought, word, look, and deed, brought under the sensitive notice of our children, is like a stone cast into the smooth expansive lake, causing circle after circle to expand until the whole is encompassed; early impressions upon the minds of children go on and on, and are never lost until the entire course of their lives is influenced and surrounded for good or for evil. (p6)

Don't forget that your children will take from yourselves their earliest and strongest impressions, and that it rests largely with you to set the metre of their tune of life for ever: in the words of Guthrie, "Moses might have never been the man he was unless he had been nursed by his own mother." How many celebrated men have owed their greatness and their goodness to a mother's training! (p11)

Don't forget the girls of the present will be the mothers of the future. Don't fail to instil early into the minds of your little girls an interest in small household duties; the most womanly of womanly accomplishments consists in the ordering, managing, and sustaining a home, as it should ever be found, clean, comfortable, peaceful, and homelike. (p22)

....

K.S. Cunningham et al, *The Young Child: a series of five lectures on child management given under the auspices of the Victorian Council for Mental Hygiene* (Melbourne: Melbourne University Press, 1931).

Melbourne was in the throes of the 1930s Great Depression when this book was published and the daily necessities of feeding and clothing their children would have been a struggle for many mothers at this time. Issued by the Australian Council for Educational Research in conjunction with the Victorian Council for Mental Hygiene, this booklet of child-raising advice originated as a series of public lectures designed to 'educate the public, parents, teachers and nurses' as to how they could best foster mental health in young children. By this time psychology was moving into the mainstream and mothers were increasingly anxious to ensure that they did not do inadvertent psychological damage in the earliest years of their children's lives.

It should be remembered that habit formation commences from birth. This means that wise handling is necessary from the beginning of life. For example, children do not naturally cry to be "picked up," but most parents very successfully teach their children to do so during the first few weeks of life. Parental inconsistency is a very serious obstacle to the formation of good habits. A child may be punished at one time and laughed at at another time for the same performance. Children are frequently expected to behave differently in the presence of visitors. The tired parent is apt to be severe on behaviour which he would regard as quite legitimate at other times. (p6)

There is nothing more sensitive than the mind of the child. Nothing needs more skilful handling; nothing is more beautiful than the happy normal development of childhood; nothing is of such scientific interest; and nothing is of greater importance for the welfare of society. (p14)

....

Zoë Benjamin, *Education for Parenthood* (Melbourne: Australian Council for Educational Research, 1944).

This child-rearing manual was published towards the end of World War Two. By 1944, Australians were confident that the Allies would win and had begun looking to the future, planning their utopian post-war society. This book is a product of its time: full of optimism that mothers could help build a better society tomorrow through the ways they raised their children today. The author, a former Vice-Principal of Sydney Kindergarten Training College, was adamant that adults should receive a formal education before becoming parents. She believed, in other words, that motherhood was a profession requiring appropriate vocational training.

Among the civilized peoples of to-day there is stirring a great creative force which is expressing itself in a desire for the building of a better world; a world that has more rational thought and justice, greater tolerance and sympathy, less selfishness and greed. The happiness or unhappiness of the new world, like that of the old, must result from the character of the men and women who are that world; a world made up of people whose fundamental needs, physical, emotional, mental and spiritual have been satisfied. If, however, children become men and women unhealthy or undeveloped in body, immature in mind and emotions, selfish, intolerant, or uncooperative in their relations with others, the new and better world will be but an ineffectual dream. In most plans for reconstruction it seems to be forgotten that success can only be achieved by making some great and fundamental change in the quality of human thought and feeling. As this, in its turn, depends primarily upon the education of the child from his earliest years, we must have not only new and better schools, but also new and better homes. For the latter, far reaching housing schemes are necessary; but this is not enough. The house is merely a shell within which is shaped the pattern of family life. It becomes a home, only when the family life is built up on a basis of mutual love, understanding and respect. As the responsibility for this development lies with the parents—a responsibility for which few of them are properly prepared—education for parenthood must be an inherent part of any plans for reconstruction.(p3-4)

Constructive discipline begins from the moment of birth by the establishment of those physical habits that are necessary for the child's physical welfare. By the establishment of these, psychological habits are being formed at the same time. Very soon after birth, the child has realized, through his mother's responses to his expressions of love or anger, whether he has the power to make her do just as he wishes, or whether he has to learn to conform to certain laws which have been made for his good. The baby who realizes that by his cries he can induce his mother to feed him before his regular hour, or by the same means can persuade her to nurse him instead of leaving him in his cot, is gaining a knowledge of his power over people which he may exploit to the utmost and which may have very serious effects upon the development of his later personality. It may, in fact, influence all his relations with others, in childhood, youth and manhood. (p33)

what play means to a child

Marion L. Faegre, *Your Child From 6 to 12* (Children's Bureau, Social Security Administration, US Federal Security Agency, 1949).

This parental advice book was published at the start of the long economic boom that followed World War Two. When we look back on the 1950s and 1960s, we think of happy, white bread families in picket fence houses in the suburbs. This book is full of Huckleberry Finn-style photos of freckled kids in overalls engaged in wholesome, outdoor play. Published by the Children's Bureau, an agency of the US federal government, this book represents an era in Australian history in which the cultural influence of the United Kingdom was beginning to weaken with the rise of American popular culture.

A child's home is the first influence on his moral development, and the one that never lets up. There he is exposed to four different kinds of help: the example of his parents; their preaching and urging; reproof and punishment when he does wrong; and the pleasant and stimulating effects of actions that result in his getting warm approval. There, in the home, the underlying capacities of the child need a chance to develop. We must be as careful not to get in the way of character development as we are about directing it. (p21)

It is a ticklish business to keep destructive fears from undermining the self-confidence of the child, a confidence so necessary to mental health. Boys, in particular, are expected to "become someone," because our society has long placed on them the task of money making and providing for the family.

They are bombarded with questions as to what they are going to "be" when they grow up; while little girls less often have this question put to them. (Something is expected of girls, too; they are expected to get married; and by the teen age some girls are fearful that maybe they won't have a chance!) (p73)

....

Ruth Quatermaine and Myra Street (eds), *Better Homes Baby Book* (London and Glasgow: Collins, 1968)

Better Homes and Gardens is a popular lifestyle magazine with global reach that was founded in the United States. This book serves a dual purpose: it is designed to both explain pregnancy and motherhood and also act as a record of infant milestones and growth. The easy-to-read publication was the bible of several generations of mothers, having been reprinted regularly from the 1940s. This edition from 1968 contains taken-for-granted assumptions about the female role as housewives that would seem old-fashioned a mere decade later, after the second wave feminist movement had challenged the pigeon-holing of women in the domestic sphere.

Occasionally a new father may feel a little resentful over all the attention the mother must pay to the baby. Part of this feeling could be jealousy but part of it may be because he would actually like to help you with caring for the baby, so you should let him. If the father is willing, he might take care of the baby while you are preparing the dinner or doing some of the household chores. With a bit of instruction, any father can give the baby a bottle, or a bath, or learn to change a nappy but do not be surprised if he objects to doing this when they are a bit dirty. His technique in changing and feeding may be unique but the baby's basic needs will have been met! (p56)

At the time of day when there is the most confusion in your home, you may find that the baby will be fussy, cry irritably and eat ravenously, as though he had not been fed all day. The rest of the day when the house is quiet and peaceful, he will sleep like an angel and go for three or four hours without wanting to feed again. ...why is the baby fussy and unhappy? In most homes, the mother is busiest as the evening meal hour approaches. She is preparing the meal, trying to straighten up the house a little and squeezing a minute to make herself pretty before her husband comes home. If there are young children, they are probably adding to the general confusion. The baby recognises this general air of tension and reacts to it the only way he knows. (p57)

....

Clair Isbister, *Should I Call the Doctor? What Every Parent Needs to Know* (West Melbourne: Sphere Books, 1979).

Jean Sinclair Isbister (1915-2008) was a paediatrician in an age in which few women were doctors. Under the name Clair Isbister she published many books on motherhood, which reached a wide audience across Australia. This book on childhood ailments reads like an encyclopaedia of illness and treatment, except for the last chapter in which the author advises parents on keeping children healthy in a broad, holistic sense.

Protection does not mean coddling the child and allowing all that is desired. There are mothers keen on what they call child psychology who say, 'My child must not be frustrated; he must develop fully and express himself,' which he proceeds to do all over the walls and furniture with complete disregard for other people's rights and property. These mothers may murmur gently, 'Darling, put down Mrs Brown's pretty vase. Mummy would not like you to break it,' as it crashes to the floor. Rapid removal of the vase and substitution of something unbreakable prior to the accident would have saved the vase and given the child the valuable knowledge that there are things that must be left alone. But the mother will stand by and see that her child gets something else. (p148-9)

When I maintain that we must find out what nature requires for health, I do not mean that we ignore modern science; far from it... Nature does not prepare people to live in a complicated civilisation; women do not know by instinct how to run a house, cook a balanced diet, or care for a baby; nature merely provides the basic urges. It is for parents to learn and apply modern scientific knowledge to the business of bringing up a family. Preparation starts before marriage, but the really effective preparation for parenthood can be done in the period of waiting for the arrival of the first baby... A factor in keeping children well is certainly the sincerity with which parents prepare themselves for the task, and research work shows that this is particularly true for the mother. (p153-4)

....

Penelope Leach, *Baby and Child* (Harmondsworth, UK: Penguin Books, 1979).

Born in 1937, Penelope Leach is a British psychologist who has written several extremely popular child-rearing manuals. This is her best-known book, first published in 1977, which has sold over two million copies around the world. Leach takes a baby-centred view which encourages mothers to trust their intuition rather than follow the rules of 'experts'. Whilst some mothers have felt relieved by her focus on simply helping babies to feel happy, Leach has been criticised for downplaying the role of fathers and for making parents feel guilty about placing their children in childcare.

"Baby and Child" is written from your baby or child's point of view because, however fashion in child-rearing may shift and alter, that viewpoint is both the most important and the most neglected.

This book looks at what is happening within your child – let's say a boy – from the moment of birth until the time when you launch him into the wider world of school. It looks at the tasks of development with which he is involved, the kinds of thought of which he is capable and the extremes of emotion which carry him along. Babies and children live minute by minute, hour by hour and day by day and it is those small units of time which will concern you most in your twenty-four-hour caring. But everything he does during those detailed days reflects what he is, what he has been and what he will become. The more you can understand him and recognize his present position on the developmental map that directs him towards being a person, the more interesting you will find him. The more interesting he is to you the more attention he will get from you and the more attention he gets the more he will give you back.

So taking the baby's point of view does not mean neglecting yours, the parents', viewpoint. Your interests and his are identical. You are all on the same side; the side that wants to be happy, to have fun. If you make happiness for him he will make happiness for you. If he is unhappy, you will find yourselves unhappy as well, however much you want or intend to keep your feelings separate from his. I am on the same side, too. So although this is a book and one that I hope you will find useful, it will not suggest that you do things "by the book" but rather than you do them, always, "by the baby".

Rearing a child "by the book" – by any set of rules or predetermined ideas – can work well if the rules you choose to follow happen to fit the baby you have. But even a minor misfit between the two can cause misery... (p16)

....

These snippets from child-rearing manuals over the last one hundred years demonstrate the fickle nature of parenting advice. Just like clothing and architecture, the maternal role has its own fashions. At times the prevailing wisdom is to adhere to strict routines, at other times the experts advocate mothers respond flexibly to their children. In certain decades mothers have been assured that 'breast is best', whilst the postwar generation associated breastfeeding with poverty, backwardness and a lack of hygiene. Some experts recommend mothers shower their children with permissiveness and affection, whilst others have warned of the dangers of overindulgence and undisciplined children.

This lightning tour of a century of advice to Australian mothers is designed to offer the reader a brief taste of what I find most valuable about history: that it shows us starkly the contingency and fallibility of our absolute truths. In other words, if we view the maternal role through an historical lens, we quickly discover that what we may think is 'natural', 'normal' or 'instinctual' for a mother is actually specific to our cultural context at this moment in time. And if we can see that things *have* been done differently by other mothers, then I hope we might feel liberated to imagine that they *can* be done differently by ourselves. There is no single, correct way to be a mum: history gently reminds us of the ridiculousness of such a notion.

Time thief
by Kasia James

I don't know how I missed the substitution. Perhaps her tiny features were not implanted in my subconscious deeply enough at that stage, as we only had a couple of days to get acquainted. Perhaps exhaustion after the birth came into it. Whatever the reason, I failed to notice that the child I took home from hospital was not my own.

My daughter was taken from me to the hospital nursery, just for monitoring, they said. I was so desperate for sleep that I was, Lord forgive me, grateful that someone else would care for her for a while. When I woke to the sound of the raucous visitors of the woman in the next bed, she was gone. Even at that stage, so soon after becoming a mother, I felt a hole where she should have been. I couldn't help staring at the plastic cot where she had lain, her round pink little face relaxed in sleep, or mewling with hunger. Instead, there was just a neatly folded white blanket, and a clipboard.

The hospital was always busy, night and day. It was like trying to rest in a train terminal, with constant announcements, people rushing about in a purposeful manner, and I was left simply to wait, hour after hour, imprisoned in my curtained cubicle. Eventually, I discovered the button next to my bed which would call a midwife. It glowed with a reassuring orange light when pressed, and finally a harried middle aged woman came to me.

"How can I help, dear?" she asked.

"My baby...where is she?" I couldn't hide the quiver in my voice. She stared at me, unbelieving.

"Did no-one tell you?" Her brown eyes widened in concern. "You poor thing! Your baby's fine, dear. She just had a bit of jaundice, and so she's having a little light therapy in the nursery. She'll be back with you in a day or so." Seeing the relief on my face, she bent over and stroked my hair in a manner which still managed to be professional, despite its intimacy. "I don't know why no-one told you! What a mess!" she cooed. "Let me give you something to help you sleep while you can."

Relieved, I tossed back the white pills she brought, and slept dreamlessly. When I awoke, I don't know how many hours later, there was a baby in the plastic crib next to my bed again. It shifted in its sleep as someone on the other side of the curtain which divided our beds laughed loudly and knocked into the IV stand. Its brows creased in consternation, and then it opened its mouth to cry, revealing pink gums. Painfully, I eased myself out of bed, and picked her up, so glad that she was back. I cradled her to my breast, and she stopped crying long enough to look up at me with unfocussed eyes. They were black. As black as the void.

A day later, sick of the constant noise of the hospital, and both of us given a clean bill of health, I discharged myself, and rode home with my new baby in a taxi. I felt both conspicuous and tremendously proud of the tiny new human I had produced. That I had made her, from her perfect miniature fingernails, to the fluff of blonde hair on her head, was a miracle to me. Stroking her astonishingly soft round cheeks, I couldn't imagine how my body had managed it.

Those early days are a blur, but I do remember the constant fight against fatigue. I sat up feeding my daughter at night, my head literally too heavy to hold. It nodded, and my neck muscles kicked in time and time again, keeping me upright, the precious child in my arms sucking greedily at my breast. She began to grow, and I took pleasure in seeing her little limbs fattening, her cheeks becoming even fuller. Still she stared up at me with those black eyes, expressionless in the night.

About the end of her second month, I started to notice whole hours disappear. I would start out in the morning, with sunlight streaming through the windows on one side of the house. Then I would feed the baby, and change her, and the next thing I knew it was mid afternoon, and the shouts of older children walking home from school would be echoing along the alleyway outside my house. I mentioned it to my friends and family when they called, but they laughed it off.

"I remember when you were small," one of them said, "You were so demanding I think your mother started hallucinating with tiredness. But it gets better - it really does."

So I continued on. There was no choice after all, than to keep responding to her cries each time she needed me. In the brief intervals when she slept, her eyelashes curled on her cheek in such a sweet way that it was almost worth it. When I looked in the mirror, the face that stared back was almost unrecognisable. My skin was grey, my eyes pouched. I splashed cold water on my face and repeated that mantra: *It gets better, it gets better, it gets better.*

Soon, it seemed as if entire days were going missing. Even the jolliest of my family started to see the change in me, and to mutter about Postnatal Depression. I heard one of them whisper to another that I seemed to have lost all track of time. When they turned up to visit, I was always surprised, and could keep no appointments. Lost in the constant demands of my child, I hardly cared. All that mattered was keeping her safe and healthy. I stopped seeing them.

One night, or perhaps it was a day, I was feeding her and staring down into the blackness of her eyes. I suppose the pose has been immortalised in countless classical madonnas. Somehow, a bee wiggled its way into my room, perhaps attracted by the odd smell. It landed on my arm, and I tried to brush it away, although I couldn't raise the energy to do so particularly forcefully. Wounded, it turned and stung, plunging its sting deep into the thin flesh of my hand. The pain was intense, and I snatched back my injured hand, eyes closed and cursing loudly.

At once, I felt the pull of my baby's eyes, and despite the pain, I returned to feeding her. But the spell was broken, at least for a moment. I still stared down at her little face, with those black eyes, but my peripheral vision was freed. I watched the sunlight stream on to the dusty floorboards, and then start to move. The pool of light brightened and extended, and then the angle changed, and the room was lit only by reflected light from the wall opposite. Still, those eyes drew me in, as irresistible as a black hole. She was sucking out my time as she fed from my breast.

Helpless, but now as aware as the caterpillar in which the parasitic wasp has laid its eggs, I could not help but to continue to care for her, even as I watched my days and weeks flash past. The baby grew fatter, but slowly, and she never smiled. The conscious loss of my time became a torture to me. I grew to hate those perfect round black eyes, their captivating stare, the blankness of the void contained in them.

I do not know how many months, how many years went by, and were sucked from me. All I remember was a banging on the door which would not go away. Zombie-like, I roused myself and unlocked it. Outside, the same middle aged midwife who had comforted me in hospital stood, a little annoyed, but health shining in her face. I could see that my appearance shocked her, for she took a step back despite her irritation.

"'Ms. Watkins? It is you, isn't it?" she asked, staring.

I nodded, tentatively.

"I called round because you left hospital without your child. I thought maybe you'd had an adverse effect to the medication or something? She's ready to come home. We've been looking after her in the nursery."

I stared down at the baby in my arms, at those black eyes. The midwife gaped at the bundle in my arms, and at me. A lock of my hair, once so shiny and red, fell past my face as I looked down at the child, and I saw with shock that it was stringy and grey.

"My baby?" I asked her, my speech sounding slurred.

"Yes, your daughter. She's a lovely child. But you need to come and take her home, or they'll have to put her out to foster care. We can't keep her much longer."

I felt the weight in my arms lift, and saw with horror that I held only a paper thin casing. Wrapped in a pink bunny rug, a chrysalis shell was all that was left of the being which I had harboured, and which had sucked away my time. The parasite, the changeling, was gone. Holes in the shiny carapace gaped up at me, blackly.

Appalled, my stomach turned, and I instinctively threw it away from me, half of me screaming that I couldn't do that to my baby. The changeling, whatever it had been, shattered like a brittle meringue against the wall. A corner of the bunny rug tore on one of the sharp shards.

Now, although I am older than I once was, I can thoroughly enjoy the time I have left with my daughter, and it seems like a half-forgotten nightmare. But when she runs to me, and hugs me tight, I know that every moment is precious. Her beautiful blue eyes shine with life.

Illustration by Ceridwen Masiulanis

Telling Tatiana
by Tara Chevrestt

My hand didn't shake as I placed the telephone receiver back in its cradle. I know this because my full and undivided concentration was on accomplishing this lone task. Place the phone back in the cradle and be calm. This could be about anything, anything at all, a false alarm, a misunderstanding, the wrong test results. Nevertheless, my hand did not shake. I was proud of myself.

It was only after I had lifted my hand from the receiver, having successfully proven to myself that I had, indeed, remained calm that I realized I had to pick it right back up again. The doctor had suggested I bring a family member with me. Who was available in the late afternoon? I had family scattered all over the tiny town of Deer Lodge, Montana, but my elderly mother couldn't drive, my father was in poor health, and I couldn't see bothering him over this. It was "women's matters", after all. Having eliminated two choices, my remaining options were my sister, brother-in-law, and my nephew. I had to nix my brother-in-law and nephew for the same reason I didn't want to call my father. I glanced at the digital clock on the oven across from where I was perched on the kitchen barstool. 4:30 p.m. My sister Bethany would be home from her job at the sawmill by now.

I said a silent prayer that she wasn't taking an afternoon nap and lifted the receiver once more. My hand—again, not shaking—automatically hit the numbers to dial her at home. Her cheerful voice answered me on the third ring. "Hello?"

"Bethany." I cleared my throat to remove the croakiness and tried again, "Bethany, are you available?"

"Ella?" Some of the cheeriness left my sister's voice. "Ella, what's up? You sound funny. What do you need?"

What did I need? Support? Someone to hold my hand? Someone to laugh with me at the doctor's mistake when it was revealed? "Dr. Smith just called me." I hesitated, struggling to find the least alarming words. "He wants me to come into the clinic and talk to him and he suggested I bring a family member."

There was a long pause before Bethany finally responded. This time, there was no cheeriness in her tone at all. Her voice was tight, concerned. "When?"

"Right now."

"Shit. I'll pick you up in five minutes." I heard the phone click on her end and normally, being the big sister, I would berate her for her use of foul language, but this time I didn't notice or care. All my focus was once again on placing the telephone receiver in its cradle. Still, I didn't shake.

I unfolded my tall 5'9 frame, all 160 pounds and forty two years of it from the barstool and went to the window to watch for Bethany's truck. Surely, it was nothing.

....

It was a fifteen-minute drive to the clinic in Anaconda. We didn't say anything on the way there. We had the windows down, allowing in the crisp September air. Usually, I would complain that the wind was messing up my short brown hair, but that day I welcomed the wind as it prevented us talking to each other. I loved talking to my sister. I just didn't want to talk about the situation we may be facing. Bethany seemed to sense this and kept her attention on the road, turning only occasionally to look at me in concern, her dark ponytail swinging as she did so.

We walked into the clinic together, one tall lanky form next to another—though admittedly her form is much more slender than my own. Bethany sat herself in a plastic-covered chair in the waiting room while I went up to the receptionist to check in. "Ella Walsh," I said my name even though the gray-haired lady behind the counter already knew who I was. "Dr. Smith called."

"He'll see you right away." The receptionist stood and briefly disappeared behind a door that led to the exam rooms. When she reappeared, the handsome Dr. Smith with the pearly-white teeth was right behind her. He was the kind of man that had me thanking God I was divorced and praying I was fifteen years younger. Any other day for any other appointment, I would be telling him about my twenty-year-old daughter, my *single* twenty-year-old daughter. Though 1,500 miles may have been between us, I never stopped thinking of Tatiana and it's every mother's wish to see her daughter happily wed. I hadn't much liked her choices in boyfriends and still tried to remedy that. As much as I hated to admit it, my daughter had a fondness for selfish, controlling men with excessive alcohol intake. Not for the first time, I wished she had been able to move north with me. I felt as though my heart were still in Texas.

"Ella, come on back here." Dr. Smith's voice was gentle as he waved me through the door. I looked back at my sister, who slowly stood from the chair, wincing as the skin on her legs unglued itself from the plastic. All three of us filed down a long hallway with pictures of mountains and calming rivers and creeks adorning the walls. I was surprised when he led us not to an exam room, but an office with a cluttered desk and two chairs facing it. A fish tank full of exotic fish stood where most doctors would have a shelf of books.

Shit. This can't be good. I borrowed some of my sister's vocabulary as I sat in one of the chairs. Bethany took the one next to me and mumbled something about wearing shorts to doctors' offices. I gripped the sides of my own chair and offered Dr. Smith a weak smile.

"Ella," he adjusted his tie nervously, "Dr. Cole called today regarding the spot on your mammogram."

I felt Bethany's hand over my own. I felt a tightening in my chest and had a sudden shortness of breath. *I'm going to die of a heart attack only to find out the spot was nothing. Sorry, Tatiana.*

I nodded at the doctor to continue, struggling to appear calm. My hands were not shaking here either. He cleared his throat and his blue eyes met my own. "It's cancer."

The world went black. I couldn't breathe. Bethany gasped. I heard an "oh no!", but I'm unsure if it came from me or from her.

How do I tell Tatiana?

A hard squeeze on my hand brought me back to earth. I blinked rapidly to clear my vision. "Are you kidding me?" Part of me still thought this could be a mistake, a misreading, a joke even. I half expected a Candid Camera man to pop into the room. Dr. Smith sadly shook his head. He then proceeded to talk to me about my options, about surgery in Butte, about mastectomy, about when chemotherapy may be necessary, and when radiation treatments were adequate.

I listened and I nodded. I visualized myself without a breast. I pictured myself bald. I imagined what my beautiful Tatiana would think of my appearance. My Tatiana was a good girl, but that may be a shock to her. I would have to prepare her before she came to visit me. I would have to tell her. How do you tell your daughter over 1,500 miles away that you may die of cancer and there's not a damn thing she can do about it? Tatiana liked to fix things. She was a mechanic, a thinker, a planner. She also had a good heart and worried about everything. What would this do to her?

I also stared at the fish in that tank. I liked fishing. I fished with my dad when I was a kid. *I need to do more of that, fishing.* After all, I had moved back up to Montana after my second divorce to be with my ailing parents. *I need to go fishing with Dad. He's not getting any younger. I need to convince Tatiana to go with us. I need more time with her before…* I decided not to finish that thought.

Dr. Smith finished explaining things to me and gave me a reassuring half hug. "Don't worry," he said. "I'm on this. I'm getting you scheduled with the surgeon as soon as possible and we are going to take care of this."

Bethany clutched my arm as though I were going to fall on my face on the way out of the clinic. I felt like telling her "the problem is in my breast, not my legs", but thought better of it.

On our way out of the clinic, a short, plump, blonde woman walked in, her left hand clutching the hand of a three-year-old girl. The girl eyed me curiously, the way children do. Her blond pigtails swung as she walked. I remembered my Tatiana when she was that age. I then felt a stab of fear deep in my gut and I almost stumbled. *Will Tatiana have a little girl like that? Will I be around to see her?*

I don't remember the drive home, nor do I remember anything my sister chattered about. Bethany attempted to fill the heavy silence in the truck with happy thoughts and sayings. She kept repeating a mantra of sorts. "Everything will be all right. We'll get you to surgery in Butte and they'll cut the lump out and it'll be just fine."

I mumbled some half-assed responses and tapped my hand on the centre console. It still wasn't shaking.

When we reached my apartment once again, I declined Bethany's offer of assistance and thanked her. I could get into the apartment on my own.

"Do you want me stay with you?" She eyed me worriedly.

I shook my head as I shut the truck door. "I need to think," I told her, "I need to get my thoughts together and call Tatiana before I tell mom and dad."

"You need to call Alex too," Bethany said hesitantly. My first ex-husband was a taboo subject, but he was Tatiana's father and I grudgingly had to agree. He needed to know. He was still in Texas and he could help her. I nodded again and offered a smile to show how brave I was.

"I'll call you later," Bethany promised, putting her truck in gear.

I felt not 46, but 86 years old as I trudged up the steps to my apartment.

....

I sat in my living room, watching the ceiling fan go round and round as I tried to get my thoughts together. My gaze wandered all over my miscellaneous knickknacks and figurines. *Tatiana bought me that blue bird. Tatiana made that frame. That's Tatiana's high school picture. She was so beautiful. How am I going to tell her? How is she going to react? Do I want to burden her with this?* So many thoughts bombarded my mind, all of them focusing on one thing: my daughter. Like anyone that becomes diagnosed with cancer, I was terrified, not for myself, but for my daughter. I had already put her through two divorces and felt as though I had abandoned her by moving across the country. Would she hate me for this, for burdening her with one thing after another?

My focus strayed to the telephone on the end table. I reached for it and my hand was not shaking. I was still calm. I hesitantly dialed Alex's number. I was amazed when he answered. Surely I showed up on his caller I.D.

"This is Alex." Upon hearing his deep and familiar voice, I had to close my eyes briefly.

"Ella?"

I shook myself out of my melancholy and decided to skip the niceties. "Alex, I'm going to be giving Tatiana some bad news and I don't know how she'll react." I clutched the receiver to my ear so hard, I felt my earring post dig into my neck. I struggled to relax my grip.

To my surprise and amazement, my ex-husband didn't respond with snarky comment, but with concern in his voice. "What's happened? Are you okay?"

I had to admit to myself that despite the failure of our marriage, Alex was a good father. I also figured his current wife must've been out of the vicinity for him to be speaking so cordially and willingly to me. Nevertheless, I needed his kind words and concern. "I have breast cancer," I began and took a deep breath before rushing to finish my explanation, "It's a lump and I'm having surgery to remove it and it may not require a full mastectomy or even chemotherapy. It may be nothing really," I finished with hope in my voice.

Alex's tone was reassuring and serious. "That isn't 'nothing' and I want more details. When is this surgery? What are your options?"

I told Alex everything I knew thus far and I felt better after talking about it. I mentioned my fears for Tatiana again. "I don't know how Tatiana will react. She's been going through a hard time and she's gonna need you to be there for her. She will be very upset."

"Tatiana is stronger than you think. She'll be worried, but she'll be supportive. She'll get through this and so will you."

I wished I could record those words to play them over and over again as needed as I hung up the phone, again with a steady hand. A new worry then engulfed me and I rushed to my little office and dug through my file cabinet. I rapidly sifted through all my folders until I found the one marked "will". I flipped through its pages and sighed in relief. It was current. One of the first things I had done after my second divorce was remedy it so that everything, what little I had anyway, went to Tatiana.

With one less thing to worry about, I paced back and forth in my kitchen. Five steps to the left, five steps to the right. *Will I see Tatiana get married?* Five steps to the left. *Who will help her with her wedding?* Five steps to the right. *Will she have enough money?* Five steps to the left and I began preparations for a cup of chamomile tea.

As I heated the water and immersed the teabag, I glanced at the digital clock on my oven for the second time that day. 7:30 p.m. It was 8:30 p.m. in Texas. Tatiana would be home from her job and would either be eating dinner or be out with friends. It being a Tuesday, I figured the former was more likely. I resigned myself to calling her. Telling her would be the hardest, even harder than telling my parents. My parents would give me support, but Tatiana would need mine.

Finally, I settled down in my living room chair again, a cup of tea to my left in its matching China saucer and the telephone in my right hand. I dialed Tatiana's number. My hand shook slightly.

After two rings, I heard my daughter's lovely and chipper, "Hey, Mom! What's up?" I choked back a sob and attempted to muffle it with my free hand. I had to press on my lips so tightly I feared I had dislocated my front teeth. "Mom?"

"Tatiana, how are you?" I finally got control of myself.

"I'm great! Work is going well. I am getting lots of overtime. I miss you though." Tatiana's words were always rushed as though she had so much to say and so little time to say it. I smiled at this.

"I miss you too, dear."

"Mom, you sound a little funny. Is there something bothering you? Is Grandpa okay?" I should have known that my own daughter would hear right through me.

"Grandpa is fine. He's having regular check-ups and cannot get around as well as he used to, but he's doing all right. He's just old." I attempted a chuckle and failed miserably.

"Grandma?"

"Grandma is fine too. Ornery as ever."

I heard silence on the other end and then the shuffling of furniture. I pictured Tatiana perching on her kitchen barstool, settling in for a long talk. I knew she would be crossing her ankles on the top rung and tucking her dark hair behind one year as she nibbled on a fingernail. She cleared her throat. "How are *you?*" She got right to the point, my girl.

I had always taught my daughter honesty and bluntness and thus, I decided it would be wise to practice what I preached. "I had a bad mammogram, Tatiana, but I don't want you to panic."

"Bad mammogram? Not panic?" I heard panic in her voice, just what I hadn't wanted.

"I have a lump. It's cancerous, but we're going to remove it. Simple procedure." Was I trying to reassure her or myself or both?

"Oh my God, Mom." Tatiana gasped. "Does it hurt? Do you want me to fly up there? I can buy a plane ticket with my overtime money. When is it? What does it entail? You know, we can beat this, Mom. It's not the end of the world."

I felt a rush of air escape me, of relief and pride. I was relieved because obviously my daughter was going to be able to handle this. She wasn't panicking as I had feared, but asking questions. I felt pride because she not only offered to spend what few pennies she had to come and help, but also because she was obviously more confident in my ability to overcome and beat the cancer than I was. I needed that confidence. I spent an hour talking to her, drawing that confidence through the phone line, across 1,500 miles. If my daughter, whom I had mistakenly thought weak and in need of support, had that kind of confidence in me, I could pull this off. I could beat this. In the end, I drew support from her.

We ended our conversation with a tearful goodbye and "I love yous" and I then sat back in my chair and for the first time that day, it really hit me. I had cancer. I could die. All this day, I had been worried about Tatiana, what Tatiana would do, what Tatiana would need, and not once had I really thought of myself. Now, knowing my daughter was going to be okay, that she would be strong enough to deal with whatever occurred, that she was a grown young woman and prepared to help and support me, it finally dawned on me. I was going to need support. I was having surgery. I was having my breast cut into, possibly cut off. I was going to go through chemo or radiation. My life was about to be turned upside down.

I picked up my now-cold chamomile tea, complete with its matching China saucer and tried to raise it to my lips. I could not do so. My hand shook violently and the mug shook uncontrollably in the saucer, the tinkling sound filling my now-too-quiet living room.

I was going to need many more pep talks from my daughter.

Author's Note:

This story is based on my mother Janet Chevrestt, who went through a very similar experience February 22, 2002. The point I tried to convey as I wrote this is that a cancer patient may be a cancer patient, but first and foremost, like my mother, they are a MOM. It's always amazed me how unselfish my mother is. Her main concern has always been her child, even when her own life was on the line. I'm pleased to say, my mother beat her cancer with surgery and radiation and has been clean to this day.

This story also appears in On the Wings of Pink Angels, *a compilation by Dawn Colclasure.*

Redefining Perfect
by Sarah Cass

One of the things I've found myself struggling with the most in the past eight years is a very selfish thought...how do I redefine my vision of my children's "perfect" lives.

When we're pregnant we all dream of our children's future. We imagine what they'll look like. Who they'll look like. The sports they'll play, the life they'll lead.

Perfect visions of a perfect future.

Our logical brains tell us not to expect all of our dreams to come true, but it's fun to imagine.

I, myself, pictured my girls as gymnasts and dancers. I was a dancer, a singer, and I hated sports. I thought my daughter would always be the same. She'd have thick, long hair like I did to play with and do up. I'd be altering her dance costumes as my mother did for me.

It would be perfect.

They were both born the image of perfect. Molly, my older daughter, had a nuchal cord and was blue, but screamed right off the bat and pinked up fast. She was gorgeous. Downy white hair, bright blue eyes, the image of her dad. Kennedy was tiny, four weeks early, my smallest baby yet...but perfect smooth, pink skin. Dark brown hair and deep dark eyes, the image of me. There was no hint of the challenges they would face, and our dreams remained intact.

As they grew and the small differences between Molly's development and my oldest child's started becoming prominent. She was frighteningly skinny, and she was not talking...at all. Then she was, but still so few words. We fought it, but eventually gave in to realize there was something different and we had to deal with it. It was our first, and we thought last, foray into the world of special needs. Speech Therapy, Occupational Therapy, Nutritionists. Our head spun with terms and treatments and fears.

Today we face a future of a mild form of autism. It will affect her future, no matter how much therapy we do now. She will face challenges unique to her, and will struggle to merge her world with ours. We will help her with this…but it's not an easy road.

Kennedy's first symptoms appeared at a young age, but we easily dismissed them. She had torticollis, but managed to overcome it when she started belly time and with some exercises. After that, we thought we were in the clear. Then the 'airplane' reflex in her arms persisted…and so we began her therapy. But she wasn't done there.

She started coughing in February of her first year of life, continued for two months straight with intermittent fevers. We finally ended up with a diagnosis of Cystic Fibrosis, and then were referred to a neurologist because of her severe hypotonia. Her left side is weaker than her right, and she has dealt with a case of tibial torsion (pigeon toe to the max). She has been in the hospital seeing more specialists and having more tests then I ever thought my children would face.

It took years for my sons hiccup to kick in. For all intents and purposes he was the 'perfect' child. He'd met all those pesky milestones right on time. Everything fell into place for him. He wanted to be a scientist for NASA (now he wants to be a doctor), and his grades reflected his ability to achieve those dreams.

Then at 13 we got hit with his diagnosis of Cystic Fibrosis as well. For a while it floored him, and us. It came out of nowhere after years of being our 'neurotypical' child.

So now I struggle with redefining perfect futures for my children. Do I think their limitations will restrict them in the long run?

Maybe.

Sometimes.

I know that with determination they can overcome anything…but I have to face that none of these goals will come without bigger struggles just to attain 'normal', much less get beyond. That's the part that pains me. Knowing that their struggles are greater. That their search is for 'normal' first, then beyond.

I will still have dreams for my children.

I will still imagine their 'perfect' futures, tempered not by their limitations, but what I know of their personalities, their lives and struggles. How they've faced what's behind them shows me how they will face what's ahead of them.

I still believe that they each have the fire to achieve whatever they dream.

Molly, she wants to be a model—and a superhero. I'm certainly not about to tell her she can't do either of those.

Kennedy has the lofty dream of being a teacher, and an author. She's go the personality and perseverance to do both.

Denver? He's given up his dreams of NASA. Inspired by his own struggles, he now wants to be a paediatric pulmonologist. He wants to work at the hospital we visit on a regular basis.

Me?

I've redefined perfect and dream solely of them being happy, strong, patient, and kind…and hope that I can give them those important virtues.

The Changeling
by Laura Evans

When Sophie first opened her eyes, six days after she was born, her mother fainted. She did not scream, and that was to her credit, for Sophie's eyes were the eyes of a sparrow.

Sophie's mother did not come round for several hours. When she awoke, she waved away the doctor's smelling salts and used her biggest ladle to beat him – and the journalist, and the man from the government – from the house. Then she set to work. She took all the glass out of the windows, and unblocked the chimney, and started to teach herself how to cook worms.

I am Mother, Hear me Roar

At first it's just a few stuffed toys and a couple of books. Then, before you know it, your house is overrun with them.

because we generally don't possess that pure nurturing instinct women seem to.

Like the primates in the zoo, many of today's mothers seem to have lost ability to raise their children instinc

Spoil Yourself
and Baby will Love it!

a:
ON-MUM FRIENDS
AND ME NOW?

ou are not giving
st possible start?

mummy sure knew ho
keep her look glamorous and tail

Are you aiming to understand the needs of your gifted child?

I started to feel a familiar fee
mother guilt! Did I cause this
I have done something differ

JRTHER...

NIUS within your child!

GPS devices which keep track of toddlers are becoming available.

Work From Home!

Born with a sweet tooth and a love of m
things, Taurean babies can be possessive
overly indulgent, so surround them wit
practical items like mini ovens, toy vacu
kitchen sets. They will get the material
they crave, and learn the value of giving

pointing, stressful
e fun you hoped?

** We need a nanny

Do you think your baby or toddler would make the perfect cover model?

LITERACY SPECIALIST CENTRE
Give your child the educational edge!

DOES YOUR CHILD HAVE WHAT IT TAKES?

Multifunction Parenting Sta

Dress them for a life of luxury in chic separates and designer du

g mum? Raising kids? Running a household

est for you? At the school
ty mums, creative mums,
rty mums, and a handful

CHAMPIONS ARE MADE, NOT BOR

en has to be the greatest responsibility of all. Everything we do no

- child's development later on.

Discover the genius in your child

BUILD TAL & SKILLS FO

ryone
in learning
2-12.

Do staff understand that your child is an individual and tailor their learning program accordingly?

I love beautifully crafted European wooden toys, which is why we chose the
offers the ultimate in sophistication
little prince or princess. This luxury furniture

e stylish little people shop

Make FUN and HEALTHY lunches for your children

Make more time yourself with th easy, nifty buys

my child prefer childcare to home?

control the mess at mealtimes?"

I happy when I meditate,
helps me learn better'

Multiple Intelligence Program

I continue to rise at
awn to make sure the entire family has all food groups
eatly stowed in insulated containers.

This neutral room is a true feast for the
and is sure to be popular with couples
have a modern, eclectic approach to in
design. Your mini he or she will love c
around, examining the old-fashioned touches a
sampling the variety of textures.

Create a sense of adventure for your little monkey with a safari-style nursery

Don't get me wrong, I'm not say
fathers don't want to do childca
we'd like to do it in short bursts,
a Saturday, followed by a round
applause. A bit like how we do c

BABY GOURMET

**LEARNING PROBLEMS?
ATTENTION DIFFICULTY?
OPPOSITIONAL, DEFIANT?**

Foods to ave
in the first y

An Open Letter to my Son
by Gemma Wright

My dear Rhys; my beautiful son,

I hope that, one day, you will understand and that you will forgive me. You won't understand why I kept falling over and "going to sleep". You will also not understand why I had to take extreme measures in order to keep you safe when you suffered a meltdown. Given the age that you were, I can understand why you thought I was deliberately trying to harm you as opposed to protecting you from harm. I am so sorry Rhys; I was doing what I needed to do in order to protect you, and there was no way to convey that to you. That is not your fault, and I think you possibly understood a little bit anyway. You have never seemed to hate or be afraid of me.

I adored you from the moment that you were born. I remember us being wheeled onto the maternity ward after your birth, and you staring out at me from what was commonly known as "The Fishtank". Such inquisitive eyes, you had – your eyes showed that you have been here before. There was some kind of ancient knowledge within you – and I could feel it.

My sweet boy. My beautiful boy. It broke my heart when I sent you to a foster carer, but what else could I do? It was only fair that you were sent to a carer who could deal with your autism without them falling over and having seizures in the same manner that I do. How could I possibly inflict my difficult life on you when yours was even harder? Rhys... I couldn't! I loved you too much to let that happen. I still do.

Everybody tried so hard to keep you safe and happy. What you are facing now is something that your loved ones knew to be inevitable – but also something that we all tried to hold off for as long as possible. What you are enduring now could *not* be prevented, but we did our best to keep this from happening to you for as long as we possibly could.

My Rhys, my Gremlin, my beloved baby boy. I embrace your beautiful soul… but I am unable to embrace what your autism has done to you. I know that you are frustrated, confused, unhappy and angry, and if I could take it from you? My gorgeous little man; I would take it from you in a heartbeat so that you could live, laugh and love in the way that so many people take for granted. Being able to sit and have a conversation with you would be everybody's dearest wish – but instead we all have to watch you struggle with words and the inability to convey emotions. Rhys, it breaks all of our hearts; not just mine.

I do not want you, my beloved son, to be in that hospital. However, I *do* want for you to have a full diagnosis and the right help and support. You are in the best place, my love, and I need for you to know that your Nana, your Auntie and your Mummy and Step-dad are all rooting for you.

You are "Nana's Handsome" and "Mummy's Gremlin", remember? We love you, my little man, and we will never stop loving you. Your happiness and the quality of your care are absolutely paramount to us.

I love you, you handsome green eyed smiling boy. I always have done and I always will. I hope that you can understand that.

Love,
Mummy xxx

Author's note: I was diagnosed with epilepsy when my son was three years old; he is now seventeen, and his profound autism has led to violent behaviours that have, in turn, resulted in his sectioning under the Mental Health Act. He is on a ward for psychologically disturbed young adults, where he is to remain until such time that he is no longer viewed as a danger to himself and others, and either returned to his foster father or placed in a residential care unit.

Letter to a Boy on his 21st Birthday
by Khaalidah Muhammad-Ali

May 16, 2012

Son,

You are older now than I was when I gave birth to you. I can honestly say that you are as beautiful to me now as you were to me then. Twenty-one years, though brief in the grand scheme of things, is still more than a lifetime for many. I feel blessed beyond measure to have shared those twenty-one years as your mom. I hope that you also consider me your friend, because you are an awesome human being.

I recall a day when you were still newborn. I was holding you in my arms after a feeding and you were falling asleep. You were a beautiful bundle of contradictions, vulnerable and innocent, yet powerful. I was struck by the most heart-rending sensation and I sobbed into the folds of your blanket. The feeling that overtook me was so great that I could never contain it, so I gave it to you, and later to your siblings. Let me assure you son that there is nothing in this world like the love of a mother for her child. Nothing.

I was too young then, at just twenty, to be afraid. I am glad for that gift of youth and fearlessness because I believe it has made me a better mother. You learned about yourself and the world through me and I was somehow pliant enough to learn from you. Seeing the world through your eyes was like pressing life through a sieve. The result was finding the best of me.

I see so much of me in you, both good and bad, no doubt due as much to proximity as to heredity. We have the same broad shoulders and erect stance, concise rhythm when speaking and that deeply innate trust in our own ability that makes others see arrogance when all we see is truth. Your love of literature and Star Trek, of good coffee and dark chocolate, of intellect and self-mastery are gifts I claim to have passed to you. That said, who could deny that careless disdain we both have for all things stagnant and abstruse that can be characterized as impatience? Like me you value fact and fiction in equal measure, but never together.

I'll share one immutable truth with you. For all of our similarities, you are better than I am in intelligence and strength and conviction (even when I think you are wrong). I can take no credit for that. You are who Allah made you. I am proud to have been the vehicle.

You used to try to impress me. As all children, you wanted to be loved and respected. You wanted your mother's approval. Look how life has come full circle. Now I want your approval. I want you to be proud of me. I received my nursing degree as much for you as for myself, that you might know that your mother is capable. And each and every story that I write is crafted with the thought that one day you will read and love it.

Before Allah I swear that were it not for life's obstacles, barring fear of doing a disservice to you, I'd give you anything and do almost anything to make you happy. But you don't need things, and nothing that I could give you at this stage will make you complete. This is because you really don't need me anymore. This dependence ended around the time you stopped giving me hugs and also when instead of looking up at me, I was looking up at you!

Within the next year or two, you will be graduating from university. I see that you struggle with decisions about your future. I wish that you didn't have to feel that pressure, but this is necessary to your growth. Continue to trust yourself and never despair about the unknown. Your life will happen, all you have to do is be present.

There are three things I wish for you as you mature:

Strong faith in Allah and the unseen. Those miracles not explained by science surely are the greatest.

Humility. It is too easy in this world to forget that we are only stardust. Being one in a googolplex isn't very unique. Never be too proud to change when change is needed.

Growth. Each day should mark the start of a different better you. Be a doer. Be a doer. Be a doer. And Allah will help, Inshallah.

We don't know how long we will stay in this world. Death approaches us all. With this in mind I wanted to tell you in clear and certain terms that I love you endlessly and without reservation. I think of you often. I am incredibly proud of you. I am your cheerleader. I am here for you as long as Allah keeps me alive and alert.

I also beg your forgiveness. In my humanity I am sometimes weak. I have not been perfect in any endeavours, including motherhood. If I have harmed or slighted or cheated you in any way, please forgive me.

Happy 21st birthday.

Mom

P.S. Some mother's warn, "Just wait until you have children. I hope they are like you." Well, I pray you do have children like yourself. It would be a blessing.

Reading my son
by Marie Marshall

My long wall full of hieroglyphs
– a lamp, two ibises, a kneeling man,
a bird, a long-tailed snake, waves
on a river, a brown sheep-fold with
a gap in its black dyke –
too late for me to find my demotic stone,
my heavy little satyr, my angular troll,
before a girl of sunlight and breeze
walks in and waltzes out with you.

Thoughts on Being a Mother
by Mary Jeavons

Elderly primigravida

I never thought much about becoming a mother. There was usually something much higher on my list. Not that I didn't want to be one; I just wasn't one of those girls who couldn't wait to have a baby.

I had already passed my mid-thirties when my husband reminded me that time was marching on. A conscious decision was required. I had never felt the need for planning much before; life had rolled along and seemed to just turn out, and I thought that was how it was meant to be. This time, I had to actually make a decision. We decided to start a family. As it happened it was a great time in our lives to do this.

Our daughter Ella was born when I had just turned 37. The doctor labelled me an "elderly primigravida"[3]. I found this highly amusing. *Moi*? Elderly? I felt young and in control.

At least being an "elderly primigravida" means you have had time for adventures when you are young. Mike and I had been together since I was 17. We had studied, then adventured through many wild places in the world on foot, bicycle and many rugged forms of transport. We had, with our friend G, renovated a hovel in Collingwood, then sold it and built another house. I had set up my business as a landscape architect, working from home, and Mike was doing well in his work. We were probably ready for a new phase even though I hadn't consciously recognised it.

New Adventures

I was also very lucky. I had no problem becoming pregnant; we subsequently had our second child William 22

---

[3] A woman older than 35 who is pregnant for the first time.

months later, so I was pretty blasé. This baby thing just happened! Knowing as I now do that women's fertility drops off significantly after around 30, this was a privilege I took fairly casually.

Being pregnant, I determined, was not going to slow me down. I kept working right till the morning my first child was due. Because Ella was a breech baby and I was 'elderly' with narrow hips, it was decided that I was having a caesarean delivery. This meant I had to arrive at my appointed time and the baby would be removed. Seemed a little soulless. Nonetheless as the workaholic I was still tapping away at my computer on some project when my husband reminded me that we needed to depart. Now. Once again his gentle reminder was required to keep me on track.

As they do, the baby had the last word anyway and my waters broke the minute I set foot in the hospital. She was ready now too. That felt better.

Parturition

There is this thing called bonding. When your baby is born you know it's meant to happen but as a new mum you aren't sure how or when. You have to negotiate carefully around this unfamiliar little creature.

When you have had a Caesar you do get more attention and help in hospital after the birth (or you used to in 1992); getting out of bed after abdominal surgery is a bit of a task and though the staff encourage you to look after the baby yourself, they do help and do some of the nappy changes and other baby maintenance for you. But in the middle of Ella's first night on earth when the staff were all busy and nowhere to be found, we needed help. She was covered in meconium (the sticky dark greenish goo that they pooh out when they are first born) and she was unhappy. I lumbered out of bed and unwrapped her and cleaned her up in my clumsy way.

I can picture to this day her little dependant frog-like body all scream and stretched-out arms. That was when we fell in love. I knew she needed me and that I was there for her. Unconditional love. Forever.

And then it all happened again when the second one arrived. No Caesar this time –his little swollen screwed up face arrived and slowly unfolded like a flower over a few days into a beautiful baby boy.

Altruism

So now she is 21 and her brother is 19 and we still love and enjoy them. In fact, they become even more fun as they get older so we needn't worry that they aren't cute toddlers any more.

Control, identity, guilt

In our western, largely affluent society, with choices of contraception, many of us do have this luxury of choice, at least about when or if we will become mothers. We like to be in control or to think we are. It's hard for many women when it dawns on us that we can't have total control and we really genuinely have to put the child's needs first.

I was always sure I could both work and be a good mother; I hired a nanny and worked from home so I was close to them. It was a strategic investment in a future (hoped for) career which meant I spent most of my income on childcare. I was in a fortunate position that my husband could keep us all on his income, but I know this is simply not an option for most families now.

Later, when I moved into an office it was only at the end of our street and I'd get up at five a.m. and work for a few hours before their breakfast. I was a stoic and felt I could manage. Largely I did, too, through good luck and a lot of hard work. I also have a very supportive and practical husband. But I know I wasn't really there for them absolutely all the time. My head was often elsewhere. I was the mother who was often late, apologising picking them up. Worrying about school holidays and how I'd be able to work. I was never the earth mother who was at home all day.

It wasn't ever about money. This was about self. My work seemed to take over my identity. This was the core of my dilemma. How could I balance my need for an identity with their very real needs for attachment, love and care, and for me actually being there for them? Are we competing with our children? Even if we didn't have children, had I got this work thing completely out of whack? (Most likely). Possibly pure selfishness. Or is it a woman thing to even question this? Do men even question the importance of their career in their lives? Is the cost to their families just a given?

Conscience

Looking back, I am probably being a little hard on myself now. Our children had lots of good detailed time with us at every stage of their lives. But I knew women who made time and space at home for extended, quality play with their kids and ours in a way I never felt able to.

Balance

Ironically my work focuses a lot on design for children and I have discovered things about brain development and related issues over the years. Attachment to significant adults is critical for children's neural pathways to develop. Especially in their early years – a window of brain development that never opens again. Children need to feel total emotional and physical security before they can become independent[4].

So many critical aspects to children's success springs from this security and attachment and the brain development it facilitates. Self-esteem; persistence; resilience; independence; curiosity, judgement, empathy. These attributes, it turns out,

---

[4] Jo Jackson King Raising the best possible child: how to parent happy and successful kids ABC Books 2010

predict children's success in life far more than academic grades.[5]

What should we do?

So with a touch of 20:20 hindsight, looking around and looking back, my gratuitous advice to the next generation of potential mothers would be:

- Think about having children and do not just let it happen. Birth control should be virtually compulsory until a conscious decision is made to have a child. *Choice*

- The child's right to have a quality, emotionally secure life with care and attention from loving adults, and to grow up free from violence and insecurity, gazumps religious rules on contraception. In my opinion.

- While we all need to balance fertility with maturity, don't have children too young. Finish your education and if you can, get some life experience under your belt. This will surely benefit your child and means you won't resent them for holding you back.

- But don't leave it too late.

- If you decide to have a child, this is a decision that lasts forever, so do not take it lightly.

- Do have children if you are able to provide an emotionally secure life for them. Emotional security is far more important than financial security but the stress of severe financial insecurity will most likely affect children's emotional development.

---

[5] Tough, Paul *How Children Succeed* Random House 2013

- Too much focus on career and money at the expense of getting down and dirty with your children, (especially when they are young) is detrimental to them and you. Make your decision and live with it.

- Find some kind of balance if you can; it's not easy, but remember you had the choice and they didn't.

- This doesn't require you to be a 'helicopter parent' hovering around them every minute. In fact they also need to be allowed to develop independence from you. This is not just an option, it's critical. Don't program their every minute, and give them time for their own self-directed play.

- Having children is as fulfilling as it is scary, demanding and exhausting. It requires you to focus on others and keeps you in the real world. It's a tough gig at times.

It creeps up on you, takes you unawares, but in dark bleak times sometimes love is all that remains –this illogical, hard to explain, force of immense power and motivation.

Unconditional love

Something Like Survivor's Guilt
for M.W.B.
by Angélique Jamail

Three miscarriages in twelve months,
The first two at seventeen days,
This latest at eighteen weeks.

A one in a thousand chance:
A fetus with sixty-nine chromosomes –
A daughter, incidentally, as they had hoped.

These are the statistics of her personal loss,
The data of her grief,
And each event a completely random tragedy.

The phone cradled next to my ear,
What can I possibly offer,
I with two healthy children not planned for?

I look at the sleeping child
Who has nursed himself into oblivion
In the crook of my arm,

And think, I have no right
To an opinion.

Filialpiety 孝
by Valerie Walawender

In Confucianism, filial piety refers to the "important virtue and primary duty of respect, obedience, and care for one's parents and elderly family members."[6]

My drawing "Filialpiety" depicts my mother at 80, and me at 20 and 55. The "egg" symbolizes the questions about identity - who am I? How am I my mother, now that I am a mother? Who came first - mother or daughter - or were we both "born" at the same time?

As I journey through womanhood and motherhood, I walk in the steps of my own mother. I gain insights into what she experienced - as the mother of infants, toddlers, school-age children, teens, and young adults. I now wonder what it will mean to me, to be a grandmother, and the mother of middle-aged adults. I remember when I was pregnant, trying to imagine what it would be like to have an infant. It is different for each age. I could not have conceived this before I walked this path.

For me, my mother was one person - a constant - but now I see that she was changing all the time, adjusting herself to what was required of her as her children grew, changed, and developed. We needed different things at different ages. Our mother rose to the occasion again and again. This very special growth process that mothers go through is unrecognized not only by their children, but by society at large. Grandmothers, mothering their adult children and grandchildren and great-grandchildren, continue the cycle, figuring out how to navigate these different relationships. All the time, they remember what it was like to mother their own children, and how their own mothers were with them.

---

[6] Random House dictionary, Random House, Inc. 2013)

How does society define a "mother"? Mothers are sometimes revered, but often times, in reality - a bit despised. They represent (to children and society) something that is a bit static, ordinary, and domestic. Living a life of "servitude," all their skills, devotion, and experience does not warrant a "professional" status or monetary reward.

The expectation of society, generally, is that, if you are a woman, you know (or should know) how to be a mother. But, of course, this is a ridiculous assumption. How we mother, depends to an incredible degree - on how we ourselves were mothered. Despite education and societal dictates, patterns by which each of us was mothered, are burned, for better or worse, into our consciousness. Sometimes we recognize the deficits, and respond with vehement determination to do better, to be better mothers than the ones we had. However - in the end, we have to acknowledge our legacy. For better or worse, we are our mother's daughters and sons. We do what we know. And what we know, intimately, thoroughly, we learned consciously and subconsciously from our first, most important teacher - our primary parent, most often, our mother.

Interview with Dr. Tram Nguyen
July 2013
by Kasia James

When I gave birth, I found that I was able to 'think' through the physical pain, and coach myself through each contraction. I came out of the birthing suite not only with a healthy baby, but also with a new respect for my body and my mental toughness. In the weeks that followed, I hit the 'baby blues' quite hard, and discovered that mental pain is much worse than anything physical. I didn't have post-natal depression: just the emotional low of going cold turkey on all those lovely pregnancy hormones. Nonetheless, I discovered the immediacy and unrelenting nature of sadness which cannot be avoided.

Mental health during pregnancy and after birth is not something which is widely discussed, but Dr. Tram Nguyen spends her professional life helping women at risk of depression, anxiety and psychosis. She works as a perinatal psychiatrist at the Royal Women's Hospital in Melbourne, Australia. Tiny and elegant, she exudes an aura of intelligence and competence, but admits that in private life, she sometimes describes herself as 'Just a Mum.'

"I don't advertise what I do, when I go out. People have strong reactions when they hear I'm a psychiatrist. Either they have an aversion - they move to the other end of the room - or they sit down and tell me about their entire family's problems!"

However, it is partly an urge to hear people's stories which drew her to the profession. "I've always wanted to be a psychiatrist," she says, "You get to make a qualitative change in people's lives, that is about the quality of living now."

Mental illness is something that is a fairly common experience amongst new mothers. Between 10-15% will suffer post-natal depression, although only 1 in 1000 will suffer the more severe and frightening psychosis. Not having had depression herself, Tram makes it clear that she can only offer a medical perspective on the issue. "I can talk about women's stories, but I don't have the authenticity of experience," she says, "It's very hard talking about mental illness because you can't make generalisations."

Unusually for the medical profession in Australia, she often sees women, and sometimes couples, in a preventative role, in addition to active treatment. The aim is to pick up patients who are at risk for whatever reason, whether it be genetic, past history, or substance abuse issues, and provide them with strategies for avoiding and dealing with the signs of mental illness before it becomes a serious problem.

"Genetics is a big risk factor," she says. "Genetics and a biological vulnerability. There are also a lot of social factors. Women in the lower socio-economic groups [for example], who may also have to deal with poverty, homelessness, domestic violence, unsupportive partners, single parenthood, adolescent parents." That said, Tram notes that middle class professional women can also be at higher risk of post-natal mental illness.

"Women coming to motherhood later, who are known for perfectionism, routine and rigidity. Teachers and nurses who have had a very structured day, for example. People who are used to things being predictable, and suddenly - it's chaos! Doctors sometimes deal better with the chaos, because they have to deal with crises professionally."

The strategies for coping may include cognitive behavioural therapy, mindfulness and meditation practice during pregnancy. Medication is often not prescribed at this stage, although each case is, of course, very individual. "Women for the most part, and it is partly the culture we have at the moment, feel like they have to be pure during their pregnancies. I often don't prescribe the first time I see someone, unless they are very depressed," Tram explains.

Purity and a wholesome and earthy approach also affects childbirth, with a natural drug-free birth held up by many as an ideal and more woman-focussed experience. Tram is more pragmatic. "A hundred years ago, half of all women died giving birth. It's not a safe experience. It's the most dangerous thing you can do as a young woman. I see a lot of women coming from midwifes who are set up for no medical intervention, and then, they have to. Doctor's don't do it to be anti-feminist. They do it because there's a baby who needs to get out safely. All those things are there for good reason."

Expectations can greatly affect the way that a woman feels about herself, and about becoming a mother. Tram explains, "I can see two women, and they will have had the same birthing experience. One will be terribly guilty and depressed, because she saw it that she had 'failed' to have a normal, natural delivery, and therefore that she had 'destroyed' her baby. Another woman may say 'Thank God I've got a safe baby. Thank God for the medical profession. How lucky am I?' It's all a question of perspective."

Unreasonable expectations, of course, relate to more than just childbirth itself. "There have been decades of myths that pregnancy is a time of protection, that all women feel bliss and happiness when they fall pregnant. No-one wants to admit that they're not happy." Can a failure to feel what we're expected to contribute to depression?

"It can contribute to women not seeking help," Tram says. "It can contribute to guilt."

"I have women who come to me and say 'I hope this baby dies,' and they mean it. There are often mixed feelings: everyone else is excited; my husband would leave me if I had an abortion." When an estimated fifty percent of pregnancies are unplanned, in many ways it would be much more surprising if everyone did feel the same way about it.

Another socially unacceptable face of motherhood is the grieving process that some women go through for their old lives. An unplanned pregnancy can completely change all the expectations a woman held for her future life, and this can take some time to get used to. "We see that very commonly," Tram agrees. " A lot of psychological work is around adjustment, and is related to loss of identity."

Teenage mothers, by comparison, can do very well in this situation. "They didn't expect to be anything other than a mother. They had no other plans. Motherhood gives them identity, that they never had before, as opposed to the women who lose their identity, and don't like the idea of being identified as just a mother. It can give you a connection to other women: it gives you some kind of status."

For those women who have had more life experience, incorporating the role of motherhood can be a challenge, and one that is currently dealt with largely in private, although there are various on-line communities and blogs which discuss matters more openly. Tram has seen many such women over the course of her professional life. She explains, "Women get resentful that they can't get back their old lives, and that can contribute to depression down the track. The work life balance is hard. I think it's always a struggle with the competing demands. Especially as you're not going to be able to compete with a male in the same position in the workforce. Even when there is greater gender equality, if you go to work, as a parent your head is still partly filled with your children. You're still waiting for that call 'He's got a fever, come and pick him up.'" Tram laughs. "You don't have that freedom that people who don't have children do."

"You can end up competing in two spheres: both at work and with other mothers, who always have their children in nice clothes!"

Part of that competition is fostered by the media. Recognising that magazines are there to sell products, rather than to help and inform women, is an important step. "I'm not sure that those magazines necessarily make those women unhappy," she muses. "Some enjoy the consumerism! For what it is. Maybe middle-class people over-think it! Again, it is about context and perception. Women who lack confidence in themselves as mothers may feel immense pressure when they see the image that is projected through magazines."

"You do get the odd article about post-natal depression or whatever, but that doesn't sell product. It's such a major industry. The amount of money people spend is stunning. Especially those people who can't afford it. It's like the less money you have, the more money you spend. I think for some people it's a sense of giving their children the best life possible, but not being sophisticated enough to understand that those material things aren't going to do it all."

"I think that it's such an individual experience, and yes, the media does set up these expectations. Stuff around natural birth and stuff around 'it's going to be the best thing that ever happens to you'. Yes, when you're out the other end, and you wake up, and there's a sleeping child there, and they smell delicious, yes, it is fantastic! It's just that you're not given the complete picture."

However, although it's never really possible to explain what the experience of motherhood is like until you are a parent, in the same way that hearing that childbirth 'hurts' is a shadow of the real thing, parenting education is beginning to change. The 'fourth trimester', meaning the three months after birth, is starting to be explored in antenatal classes around the country. "It's about the hard slog, the sleepless nights, the physicality of feeding," Tram explains. "That it takes forty minutes to feed, and then to settle, and that you'll not have more than two or three hours, if you're lucky, of uninterrupted sleep. You get that now. But I'm not sure how useful it really is to also say, 'You have a ten percent chance to getting post-natal depression.'"

There is a chance that by giving parents information about depression and mental illness before they need it, that these conditions may become a self-fulfilling prophecy. Tram feels that with an issue like this one, there is a big difference between doing something universally to everyone, versus targeting women who are at risk. "Are you just creating unnecessary harm and worry? People who are already anxious may become more anxious. You could be contributing to the problem. You could end up being seen as the scrooge who wants to rain on someone's parade, just because they're happy during pregnancy. I would actually like to do a survey on women, and not necessarily just the ones that I see, to get a sense of how much information they would like."

Tram stresses that there is a single mental health message which should be getting out to women. "What's important to know is that if something goes wrong, you can talk to someone about it. That's the only message that I think should be out there, and don't feel guilty about looking for help."

The stigma around mental health issues stems largely from fear of the unknown, but this attitude, combined with the social unacceptability of not being happy during pregnancy or with a new baby, are major contributors to women hiding their depression.

"Beyond Blue has done very well there in reducing this stigma. It's people like Brooke Shields coming out and telling her story, and Jessica Rowe in Australia. On the Beyond Blue website[7], people post their stories. Some of them are blogs, some are videos. High profile people coming out though, like celebrities: it's more useful than some textbook saying 'This might happen, that might happen.'"

---

[7] http://www.beyondblue.org.au/connect-with-others/personal-stories

A huge problem when thinking about depression in general is that people don't necessarily realize that they are depressed. A single issue can be overwhelming, and thinking about it can be all consuming. Obviously with a new child in the house, the baby itself can seem to be the issue. One might assume that at such an obviously stressful time, people might be more aware of a woman's fragility, but this is not necessarily the case. Tram explains, "It depends on whether or not people want to see it. Often partners don't want to. It's a sense of loss for them. You lose your partner for that period. They're not the person they were. Having a partner who is depressed is really hard work. When you have a child you end up sole parenting. Partners often hope that it is a short phase and that things will just go back to normal – that they will have their wife/ partner back. Sometimes this contributes to a delay in getting help. Also, that when you're in it, it can be so hard to see clinical depression and anxiety for what it is."

The effects on children have been extensively studied, but the results are not straightforward to interpret. Part of the reason for that is the difficulty in separating biological and genetic imperatives from upbringing: the old Nature vs. Nurture debate. "It's blurry, because it's also treated versus untreated, and how long a parent has been depressed for," Tram says. "You can see that if the mother is very depressed, then the baby may also look depressed. What we see is babies that don't cry, that are gaze avoidant, that are difficult to settle, that lose weight like they've got something physically wrong with them – even though there is no identified medical cause. They're just sad, because Mum's sad. Sometimes it helps if Dad is available, or Grandma is available, and can smile at them and so on."

With an intense period of brain development happening in infancy, you might expect that a withdrawn or depressed parent would have some effect on a child's natural mental growth. However, this is not always the case. "Some studies show that if it's untreated for long enough, that babies, later on, are not as cognitively acute. Some of that is not getting enough stimulation. It can delay language acquisition. Mum's depressed, so she doesn't talk. She can't even make eye contact with you. She's just lying in bed. After she's fed you, she'll just put you down. Dad might be at work all day. You're just not getting that stimulation. The difference is between that and speaking with a high pitched voice, which is what babies need, and a parent who will read to you every day, talk to you while Mum's feeding you.

"It doesn't mean that babies can't catch up! Depending on which part of development and so on, and how long depression goes untreated. They can catch up."

Women who come through a mental illness can also 'catch up.' "Most women come out stronger," opines Tram.

Even without any kind of medical issue, parenthood is a tough gig, and Tram feels that just as much as any of us. "Sometimes I say I'm 'Just a Mum'. I've got two kids. I can say all these things, but that doesn't mean that I feel free of pressure. Perhaps more so because I'm meant to be the person who knows what they're doing!' she laughs. "For example, people ask things like 'You've got kids, how much do you work? Can you work and be a successful Mum?' And yes, I do work, and I cook dinner six nights a week, and no, we don't have a cleaner. And yes, I do struggle with the work-life balance."

"The thing is, at the end of the day, your kids will tell you whether or not you're doing a good job. We don't have a culture that passes on instinctive mothering any more. Mothers and aunts don't sit around and talk about their birthing experience, and about parenting. So now women totally lack confidence in it. They're looking for something to tell them the right way to do it."

"For me, I had the confidence to say, 'You know what? I think I'll be able to work this out. If it doesn't work, it doesn't, but I think I'll be able to work this out.' If your kids are growing and they're healthy and happy, then you're doing fine. And of course, if you're enjoying it yourself – not necessarily all of it, but most of it, most of the time."

A teenage pregnancy
by Marie Marshall

> You, a year my senior, were
> too cool to talk to me, until
> the day you rose like bread,
> cupped like a pitcher-flower
> catching rain, and began
> a light like heated silver;
> not that we spoke much
> – we sat and ate lunch together,
>   sometimes sharing the neck
>   of a sweet bottle –
> or I would have told you I was
> bathing in your glow, and
> wanted to kiss you
> for your magic.

My Real Mother
by Judith Dickerman-Nelson

My mother grew up near Davis Square on Highland Avenue in Somerville, Massachusetts. Her father worked in furniture, reupholstering chairs and couches, fixing a spring, sewing a seam, making a living while her mother kept busy raising children. There were three girls and six boys.

My mother was the youngest daughter and ironed clothes for her older sister Margaret, the one they called Queenie - I suppose because she was like a queen bee they all worked for. In pictures from someone's wedding, my Aunt Margie looks regal, her pillbox hat and white gloves the finishing touches to her smart outfit.

I remember when I was a child and we went to Little Neck in Ipswich to visit my aunt and cousins. My mom and her sister laughed over summer cocktails, and the men drank their beers while the children sipped on sodas and ate chips with the smell of salt in the air.

I have one brother and one sister, so I couldn't understand how my mom kept track of her siblings' names. Wasn't she confused? Especially when each boy had a name and a nick name? Roland was Porkie, George was Mucca, someone was Greenie, and then there was Quack who was sometimes Frank. Chickie was my Godfather, and it seems I've forgotten one.

I never met any of my grandparents who were all dead before I was born, but there's a picture of my brother - just a toddler - in his Papa's lap. My grandfather is wearing a suit that seems gray while my brother has a button down shirt with suspenders to hold up his little shorts. When I look at old black and white photos, it is like staring down time, tumbling in my mind to a place I can only imagine.

My mother told stories about her own mom who welcomed strangers into their home. It was the depression and hobos rode the steel rails looking for work and something to eat. My mother's mom believed you could always throw another potato into the pot, always find a way to feed a hungry mouth.

But there must have been a shortage of beds. Because during this time, my mother was shipped off to live with her sister - not Queenie, but Charlotte my Godmother whose first husband was a policeman. He used to get drunk and abuse his family. Mom didn't tell me too much about this time except that they feared his gun and that the yelling could go on into the night. I imagine him coming home from work angry and sullen and how the family would all put on poker faces, expressionless stares meant to appease his passions and keep them safe in God's hands.

When Mom went back home, her neighbour would watch her walk to the bus stop to go to work. He was a few years her senior, and when he asked her out she said no. World War II had started, and that man, my father, joined the war. He wanted to fly planes, but when he bounced one down the runway on his first test landing, he had to choose another path. He became a navigator and learned to read the stars, participating in numerous bombing sorties. He was part of the Great Generation - silent and stoic. He held his stories inside, harsh memories like sad secrets he couldn't share.

After he returned, my parents started dating, and at some point they broke up. The particulars of their romance remain a mystery, but I know they got back together. Because in April of 1953, they were married. My mother was 28 and a half, and my father was already thirty-one. And they wanted to start a family.

When they couldn't get pregnant, they consulted doctors. My mother went into Boston and became a guinea pig for early fertility treatments. Doctors in Boston put her on an early birth control pill. The idea was that if ovulation was suppressed for a few months, somehow a woman's body would more vigorously produce eggs after stopping the pill.

In those studies, in fact, thirteen women out of eighty did become pregnant.

I wonder if this was the time my mother had her one pregnancy. I was sixteen and pregnant when she told me that she'd been pregnant once. We were sitting at the kitchen table, smoking cigarettes and drinking tea. She told me she had a miscarriage, and with a baby growing inside of me, it was hard to comprehend what that loss must have been like.

I felt sad for my mother, but part of me was glad. If she had brought that pregnancy to term, she and my father would have had no need to adopt me, and my sister, and my brother. We always knew we were adopted because my parents read the book *The Chosen Baby* by Valentina P. Wasson to us. I loved to hear the story about a couple waiting for their special baby and how they rushed to the adoption agency to scoop their new child into their arms. The parents in the book adopt two children, and it's clear how special their babies are to them.

My mother and father adopted three of us, and I know they considered us their chosen babies. But I always wondered about the women who gave us up. It's hard to explain how you can feel completely loved by the parents who raised you while still feeling abandoned and unwanted by those who gave you away. I wrote this poem to explore these feelings:

Select Features (first published in the journal *Red Brick Review*)

I wonder how my mother felt the last time
she held me, after she'd signed forms releasing
me for adoption. Did she try to memorize my face,
touching my cheek and chin, or was she thinking
of how she'd planned to take me back, keep me
in her room where I would be her own porcelain
doll: blue eyes, pink lips, and short wisps

of strawberry-blonde hair? She'd put me in a bassinet
by her bed, and she wouldn't have to say good-bye
again. There'd be no more walking four blocks
to the bus stop each day she came to see me,
and I like to believe she came every day
even though she was still bleeding,
stitched and sore. She'd travel miles, trudging
through snow if she missed the bus, never complaining
because she came to hold her daughter
and that was enough.

I don't really know what happened;
Catholic Charities gave little information then,
but my adoptive parents told me what they knew;
the mother was Catholic, twenty and unmarried,
the father was the son of a Protestant minister,
and I was born in November. It's a short history,
but it has important elements of a good story:
the essential star-crossed lovers, the families torn
apart by the affair, a pretty baby to patch
the tears, and then they'd all live happily ever -
ever - but the after didn't follow.

Perhaps when my mother said good-bye
she concentrated on my baby smell, pressing
her nose into my hair, inhaling, as if by taking
my scent she could carry some piece of me.

Years later, when she held other infants
it would seem like a perfumed letter in her pocket
opened, bringing her back to 1962 -
the last time she held me in her arms.

   I could only imagine the emptiness she must have felt.
And I often wondered if she thought of me. Like on my
birthday. Or at Christmas. And what about on Mother's
Day?

So, in reality, I had two mothers. The one who gave me away, and the one who chose to get me from Catholic Charities. It's no wonder, then, that when I was sixteen and pregnant, I balked at my fiancé's parents attempts to have me either abort my baby or to give him up for adoption. I was already in love with the small child I was carrying inside my body. There was no way I would get rid of him. No matter the cost, I would bring him into the world and raise him.

Part of me knows that giving a child up for adoption must take great love. To recognize that you cannot properly care for the baby carried in your womb and to love that infant enough to entrust her care to strangers is, surely, a huge sacrifice. But it is not something that I can really understand. Still, my birth mother gave me the gift of my parents by surrendering me for adoption, and for that I am eternally grateful.

Sometimes, when people find out I am adopted, they ask me questions about my "real" mother. My real mother's name is Ruth Dickerman, the woman who raised me. She is the one who comforted me when I was a child and woke in the night, letting me crawl into bed with her and snuggle by her side. She is the one who cooked my meals, saw me off to school, bathed me and dressed me, read stories at night, and kissed me good-night, wishing me "happy face in the morning" - her bed-time blessing meant to remind me to always greet the world with a smile.

She adopted her children, so she didn't get to have the experience of giving birth. But she was by my side when I gave birth to each of my boys. She held my hand, she wiped my brow, and she watched as her grandsons emerged from my body. For a long time, I believed that creating a child and giving birth was one of the few moments where we are able to actively participate in a miracle. And I do believe that birth *is* a miraculous event.

But now I am convinced that love is the true miracle. Love is the saving grace amid the chaos of this world - and it is found in a thousand places in each day. When we reach out to another human being in compassion, we participate in the miracle of love. And perhaps one of the most profound examples of love is found when a mother rocks a child in her arms and sings a quiet lullaby.

Tin-Can
by Sandra Danby

Ta-da-da-paaa-da.

Ta-da-da-paaa-da.

The 10.31 passes at 10.32.

Sheila does not raise her head, but the voice is hers. "Ta-da-da-paaa-da. Ta-da-da-paaa-da-paaaaaaa."
She giggles as if hearing the punchline of an excellent joke. She always liked the ones about bosomy ladies at the seaside, the saucy postcards with fat ladies with pink cheeks wearing voluminous bloomers and a flower tucked behind the ear. Sheila's easy-wash acrylic pink cardigan stands proud of her hunched shoulders, as if the wool has more strength to stand up on its own than she does.

"Ta-da-da-paaa-da. Ta-da-da-paaa-da-paaaaaaa. Shuttershudtershutshut…"

Her lips barely move, her fingers pluck at invisible bits of fluff on the knees of her easy-wash black polyester trousers.
A hand takes hold of Sheila's questing fingers, gently, stilling their motion. "It's okay, Mum, your trousers are neat and clean. You look pretty today."
"What?" The voice that barks must come from the mouth of a sergeant-major, not this frail birdlike lady who is Meg's mother. The frail birdlike lady who is glaring, unseeing, at the stranger sitting beside her, the stranger who is too close, who will hurt her, who wants to steal from her. "You c**t, you whore, you…"

Meg quickly drops the questing fingers and slowly leans back in her chair, wanting to enfold her mother in a hug but fighting that need because it is her own need. To her mother, the hug would be an attack, an assault, to be defended. The look of anger in Sheila's eyes does not belong to Meg's mother, the mother who hugged her when Billy the guinea pig died, the mother who marched into school to complain about dirty toilets, the mother who cried as she watched Meg marry Martin.

Not the mother who now closes her eyes again, muttering, her fingers moving to her left knee. "F**king go, go, f**k away, go…"

Meg closes her eyes, and wonders how they both came to this place so close to the railway track that the building shakes four times every hour as the tinny train rattles over the points.

Ta-da-da-paaa-da.

Ta-da-da-paaa-da.

Shuttershudtershutshut…

Living Backwards
by Judy McKinty

I feel like I've lived my life backwards.
Married at 19
Pregnant at 20
Three kids under 3
Living at the other end of the state
Away from my home
Away from my parents
Away from my friends
Away from the person I was becoming.
And all for love.

No longer me – instead, 'Mum'.
Trying too hard to be a 'good mother'
And a 'good wife',
This child bride.
Adapting to different rhythms
That are not my own.
Taking my cues from others –
Mothers with more experience.
Not necessarily a good thing.
It depends...

Keeping the kids clean, fed, healthy, well-behaved
With a mixture of love and yelling.
Mostly yelling, it seems.
Moulding them into 'good kids',
Such hard work.
They keep trying to squeeze out of the mould
Along the edges.
To assume their own shape.
But I squeeze them back in
Because I don't know any better.

That was at the beginning of my life.
Now I'm at the other end.
Still 'Mum', still 'wife', but also 'Nanna'.
What a difference.
What a joy
To be as close as I can be to them,
My grandchildren.
Where was all this patience, this wisdom
This easy-going-ness
When mine were young?

My children share their own with me
With unconditional love.
We talk, plan, laugh, cry, agree, disagree –
Parents together.
There are no moulds here,
No squeezing, squashing, stifling.
Each child free to become the person they will be.
And I am part of this
Because I am now old and wise.
I feel like I've lived my life backwards.

Contributors

Maureen Bowden is an ex-patriate Liverpudlian living with her musician husband on the island of Anglesey, off the coast of North Wales, where they try in vain to evade the onslaught of their children and grandchildren. She writes for fun and she has had several poems and short stories published. She loves Rock 'n' Roll, Shakespeare and cats.

....

Kitty Brody. Mother of two, grudgingly in my late 20s, living in London; the best place in the world when it's not raining, snowing, or boiling hot. Wearer of short shorts, and occasionally Mum Jeans. Faux librarian, Feminist, and occasional writer who blogs at www.apencilskirt.wordpress.com

....

Sarah Cass's world is regularly turned upside down by her three special-needs kids and loving mate, so she breaks genre barriers, dabbling in horror, straight fiction, and urban fantasy. An ADD tendency leaves her with a variety of interests that include singing, dancing, crafting, cooking, and being a photographer. She fights through the struggles of the day, knowing the battles are her crucible and though she may emerge scarred, she's also stronger. While busy creating worlds and characters as real to her as her own family, she leads an active online life with her blog, *Redefining Perfect* (www.redefiningperfect.com), which gives a real and sometimes raw glimpses into her life and art.

....

Tara Chevrestt is a deaf woman, former aviation mechanic, dog mom, writer, and editor. You'll never see her without her Kindle or a book within reach. As a child, she would often take a flashlight under the covers to finish the recent Nancy Drew novel when she was supposed to be sleeping.

Tara is addicted to *Law & Order: SVU,* has a crush on Cary Grant, laughs at her own jokes, and is constantly modifying recipes and experimenting in the kitchen. Her theme is *Strong is Sexy*. She writes about strong women facing obstacles—in the military, with their handicaps, or just learning to accept themselves. Her heroines can stand alone and take care of themselves, but they often find love in the process.

You can connect with her on:

www.facebook.com/pages/Tara-Chevrestt-Sonia-Hightower

or follow her blog at www.bookbabe.blogspot.com.au/

....

Sandra Danby grew up on a small farm on the edge of the Yorkshire Wolds. She wrote her first adventure stories at the age of four, filling home-made magazines with her writing and drawing. After more than 30 years as a journalist, she returned to her first love: fiction. Now she writes five days a week, dividing her time between Surrey and Andalucía, Spain. She is currently working on Connectedness, her second novel about Rose Haldane, family history detective. Ignoring Gravity, the first in the series, is published online at www.sandradanby.com. As well as writing fiction, she blogs about her life in Spain at www.notesonaspanishvalley.com and has learnt how to swear in Spanish.

....

Judith Dickerman-Nelson is a graduate of UMass Lowell and Emerson College. She has taught writing at the high school and college level and has attended Bread Loaf Writers' Conference and the Vermont Studio Center. For 15 years, she worked at the Cambodian Mutual Assistance Association in Lowell, Massachusetts, where her love for the Cambodian community grew. She has travelled to Cambodia, studied and performed traditional Cambodian dance, and begun to learn the Khmer language. Her poetry and prose has appeared in numerous journals and anthologies. *Spirits Dancing Into Light* is her first book of poems. Her memoir/novel, *Believe in Me: A Teen Mom's Story*, was published by Jefferson Park Press in 2012. She lives in southern Vermont with her husband and has two grown sons.

....

Laura Evans began writing while studying seventh-century Anglo-Saxon horology at university. She turned to short stories in 2011 as a way to pass an unreasonably long commute; this soon evolved into the downright foolhardy ambition to complete 1,000 stories of 100 words each, at a rate of one per day. Now about two thirds of the way through, you can follow the project's progress at www.vforvignette.com.

....

Judith Field was born in Liverpool and lives in London. She is the daughter of writers, and learned how to agonise over fiction submissions at her mother's (and father's) knee. After not writing anything more creative than a shopping list for about 30 years, she made a new year resolution in 2009 to start writing and get published within the year. Pretty soon she realised how unrealistic that was but, in fact, it worked: she got a slot to write a weekly column in a local paper shortly before Christmas of 2009 and that ran for a several years. She still writes occasional feature articles for the paper.

She has two daughters, a son, a granddaughter and a grandson (who inspired her first published story when he broke her laptop keyboard. Unlike in the story, a magical creature didn't come out of the laptop and fix her life). Her fiction, mainly speculative, has appeared in a variety of publications, mainly in the USA. She speaks five languages and can say, "Please publish this story" in all of them.

Her work has been published in many places, including *The Lorelei Signal, Fiction on the Web, Iridium Sound, Fabula Argentea and Luna Station Quarterly* ezines.

She is also a pharmacist, freelance journalist, editor, medical writer, and indexer. She blogs at www.millil.blogspot.com

....

Christa Forster is a writer, teacher and performer. Her work has appeared in a variety of journals, most recently *Intellectual Refuge* and *Zocalo Public Square*. She blogs at www.christaforster.com and www.antilogicalpedagogical.wordpress.com. She lives in Houston, Texas with her husband and two children.

....

Sabrina Garie is on a journey to create the most kick-ass heroine romance fiction has ever known and the hero who can take her. A believer that big, audacious goals spice up life, she relies on coffee, red wine and laughter to make those goals (and her characters) come alive. When not at the computer, she wrangles vegetables and extra helpings of homework into her star-spangled, fashion-loving progeny, kowtows to a fat cat and reads, a lot. For years of her youth, she wanted to be an astronaut, just to see what's out there. So now, she just makes it up herself.

Since it is more fun to travel in packs, come along for the ride. You can find her on her blog sabrinagarie.com, Facebook: www.facebook.com/SabrinaGarieAuthor or Twitter: @sabrinagarie.

....

Angélique Jamail's writing has appeared in more than two dozen publications: most recently, an essay in *Pluck* magazine and poetry in the Mutabilis Press anthology *Improbable Worlds*. In 2011, her work was highlighted as a finalist in the New Letters Prize for Poetry. Find her online at her blog (www.SapphosTorque.com), on Facebook (Angélique Jamail, Author), on Twitter (@AngeliqueJamail), and at www.AngeliqueJamail.com. She also writes fiction, mostly magic realism and fantasy, and currently teaches English and Creative Writing to grades 9-12 at The Kinkaid School in Houston, Texas, USA.

....

Jennifer James is a Northeastern Ohio native who studied under Sean Thomas Dougherty at Cleveland State University. Wife, mother, companion to a long suffering, ancient, black lab, and tolerated human slave of an attack cat. A multi-published author of erotic romance in several sub-genres, she loves to fish, make jewellery, and believes 42 is the answer to the question. She's not sure her English degree is good for improving fishing skills, but it's come in handy with learning how to tell a good story. You can find her online at www.authorjenniferjames.com, although she hates website maintenance, and admits her site needs updating.

....

Kasia James lives in Melbourne, Australia, with her son, a hydrologist, and a big black cat called George. She works as Landscape Architect, but writes primarily speculative fiction, and has been published in various magazines and journals. Her novel, *The Artemis Effect*, was released in 2012, with a collection of short stories to be released in 2014. If you have an urge to do so, you can connect with her at her blog (www.kasiajames.wordpress.com), on Twitter (@KasiaJames), or Facebook (www.facebook.com/pages/Kasia-James-author)

....

Mary Jeavons is a registered landscape architect with over 25 years' experience in landscape architecture and the planning and design of children's spaces of all kinds.

She grew up on a farm in the bush on the central coast of NSW –formative years that shaped a deep interest in nature, landscape and being outdoors. Mary is a strong advocate for play in natural settings, inclusive play environments, collaborations with stakeholders, and design that fosters and supports social interaction in communities.

She is the director of Jeavons Landscape Architects, a specialist firm based in Melbourne which has developed a core of expertise in the design of accessible, inclusive outdoor play areas in early childhood and early intervention centres, school grounds, public parks and gardens, and hospitals and therapeutic environments.

She has two children, and she and her husband Mike are keen cyclists and travelers, frequently combining these two interests.

....

Jessica Kennedy is the mama of three wildly amazing children. They smell of lavender, have hilarious one liners, smile like the whole world is looking and sometimes drive their mama crazy. She blogs at www.mamaconfessionals.wordpress.com, about which she says: "*Mama Confessionals* was created on a feeling. A feeling of disconnect. A desire to feel as a part of a whole. I knew as a new mom I needed a space where I could come and know I was not alone on my journey. I wanted to feel and hear the other foot soldiers of motherhood. I wanted a space where my words were heard and someone would understand. I had a strong desired to hear 'I know, me too!' I needed a space to come online and find endurance, hope and connection. I wanted to be able to join together with marvelous women who fight their own battles every day, to share our power and wisdom.

I wanted to contribute to this outstanding anthology to connect us with stories. I wanted to help tell the story of honest mother hood. We hide from the dark but only with the dark are we able to see the true spectacular beauty of the light."

....

Judith Logan-Farias is an artist based in Ballymena, Northern Ireland, although she spent nine years living in Chile. An artist and illustrator, she works in various media, in a style that has been described as a mix of naive, figurative and semi-abstract. She is inspired by Nature, pattern, colour and designs, and loves to sketch from life when her three young children will permit her to. She not only produces beautiful prints and artwork, but has also done book illustrations and album covers.

You can find her at: www.judithlogan.blogspot.com.au, and on Facebook at www.facebook.com/judithloganartist

....

Judy McKinty is married with three adult children and four grandchildren who are among her favourite companions. In her other life she is a children's play researcher who has been collecting and sharing children's games, rhymes and other playground activities since the late 1980s. One of the things she enjoys most is swapping jokes with her grandchildren, because she's now too slow to play Chasey and Duck Duck Goose.

....

Marie Marshall is an English-born Scottish author, poet, editor, recluse, and molehill-mountaineer, who started her writing career when already in her forties. In the past ten years she has had more than two hundred and thirty poems published in magazines, anthologies, and collections worldwide. The strangest places her poetry has appeared are perhaps on the wall of a cafe in Wales, and etched into an African drum in the New Orleans Museum of Art. In Scotland she is known for macabre short stories. Her first novel, *Lupa*, was published in 2012, and her second, *The Everywhen Angels*, is scheduled for publication in time for Christmas 2013. Marie was on the editorial team of *Canadian Zen Haiku* and *Sonnetto Poesia* magazines, and is deputy editor of the latter's swan song, the major anthology of sonnets *The Phoenix Rising from its Ashes* (also due out by the end of 2013). She is editor of the e-zine *the zen space*. Marie's web site is at www.mairibheag.com

....

Ceridwen Masiulanis is a sculptor who lives in Melbourne, Australia, who has lived on three continents. When not tangling with her extensive garden or wielding her chisels, she is being exhausted by her grandson.

....

Betty Ming Liu is a New York-based blogger, journalist and artist who teaches journalism at New York University and many other colleges. Her 15-year newspaper career includes an 8-year stint at The New York Daily News as its nationally syndicated columnist on diversity and the immigrant experience. Betty is currently working on a how-to book that will be her answer to the world's tiger moms and a resource for survivors that draws from her life as a single, divorced working mom.

Keep in touch with her by subscribing to her blog (BettyMingLiu.com) and following her on Facebook (www.facebook.com/BettyMingLiu) and Twitter (@BettyMingLiu).

....

Khaalidah Muhammad Ali. Of herself, Khaalidah says: "I grew up in New Haven, Connecticut but transplanted to Houston, Texas more than twenty years ago. I've been married to my husband for more than twenty years and have three amazingly intelligent and artistic children who outstrip me in every way possible. I work as an oncology nurse at a world renowned cancer centre in Houston, Texas. My greatest love, aspiration, and avocation is writing. I am a Muslim and I pray five times a day. I like video games, anime/comics, reading, walking, Wii boxing, horror movies and zombies, and hanging out with my children. I sew and along with my husband, I maintain a pretty spectacular organic garden in my backyard. I am an indie author with one published novel entitled *An Unproductive Woman*."

Website: www.khaalidah.com
Twitter: www.twitter.com/#!/khaalidah
Facebook: www.facebook.com/KhaalidahMA

....

Dr Carla Pascoe is an historian with a particular interest in the everyday and intimate details of our lives. She works as a Research Fellow at the University of Melbourne and as a consultant historian, and sits on the Reference Committee of the Australian Children's Folklore Collection at Museum Victoria.

Her publications have investigated the experiences of children and women in the past, including changing attitudes towards menstruation across the twentieth century and the childhood landscapes of baby boomers. She has published two books: *Spaces Imagined, Places Remembered: Childhood in 1950s Australia* (2011) and *Children, Childhood and Cultural Heritage* (2012). Since becoming a mother to Sofia in January 2013, she has begun researching the changing historical experience of motherhood in Australia.

....

Cheri Roman is a writer, editor, teacher, wife, mother, grandmother and friend, in whatever order works best in the moment. Most days you can find her on her blog, *The Brass Rag* (www.thebrassragcnr.wordpress.com), or working on the next novel in her fantasy series, *Rephaim*. Cheri lives with her husband and two Chihuahuas in St. Johns, Florida.

....

Valerie Walawender is an Art Facilitator and Consultant, and has presented to workshops and conventions across the U.S.A. She is the creator of *Faces in the Crowd*, an art-based diversity and violence prevention tool, which was endorsed by Arun Gandhi, grandson of Mahatma Gandhi, as "one of the best diversity/violence prevention tools in the country," and later adopted by the M.K. Institute for Nonviolence in Memphis, Tennessee, as part of their programming.

Having created numerous community initiatives, Valerie's career includes work as a documentary photographer; Director of Advertising for a national manufacturing company; Exhibit Specialist for the Miami Zoo; Guest

Curator of Folk Arts for Castellani Art Museum at Niagara University; and Executive Director of a regional art gallery. Active as a folklorist, Walawender also enjoys success as a puppeteer, muralist, etched glass sculptor, and inventor.

    She lives with her husband and their two sons on a hundred year old farm in the fruit belt of Western New York.

....

Gemma Wright was born in The Cotswolds, but now lives with her husband in East Anglia, England. She works closely with Epilepsy Action UK - having appeared on a short video by the charity that was put together for the 2012 Paralympics - and is a strong advocate for the awareness and acceptance of both epilepsy and autism. She writes at www.rosewinelover.com and is also a voluntary entertainment journalist for *What Culture*

....

Rhyannon Yates is a writer, a blogger, Whovian, and poster of witty status updates. Typically, she can be found as a contributor to *The Brass Rag* (www.thebrassragcnr.wordpress.com) or working on one of her three novels, switching genres as the fancy takes her. Rhyannon currently resides with her husband, two daughters and cantankerous cat in Florida.

Discussion Questions

Birth

Pregnancy and the birth of a baby change a woman's world fundamentally. There is no going back. The experience itself is an integral part of the becoming a parent.

- Was your birth experience what you expected? Explain.

- What did your experience with pregnancy and birth tell you about the mother you are becoming?

- How has your infant surprised you? What personality traits is she or he already manifesting?

Life lessons on being a mother

Once you find your bearing, motherhood evolves into not only a physical redesign of your world, but a mental and psychological one, with assumptions, world views and expectations about life being continuously reshaped.

- How has having a child changed your life? Discuss it through all lenses—gain and loss.

- What family rituals have you established as part of the parenting role? Do rules and rituals matter and why?

- How does parenting differ between mother and father, and what impact does that have on family dynamics?

- How do you balance work, motherhood and other family/community obligations? What toll does that balance take on you?

Identity Challenges

Having children can fundamentally alter how we see ourselves and our place in the world and how others see us. It can layer on duties and responsibilities that have to be balanced with our own, often volatile egos and sense of self.

- How do you feel your identity has changed since having children?

- How has that identity altered as your children have grown?

- What do we owe to our children? Is there a limit?

External Pressures on Mothers

Women face a lot of external pressures—from books, media, family and friends, community groups, politicians—that is always telling them how to be a mother, and by definition how not be one. Those pressures often dig deep, undermining our confidence, and overwhelming us with conflicting information.

- How do you think society sees motherhood?

- To what degree do you agree with that perception?

- How have these external perceptions affected your own experience?

- How do you feel society has put limits on your parenting and how have you dealt (or not dealt with it).

- How do you keep negative pressures at bay?

- Which influences have been positive and useful?

Adapting and Accepting Change

Often, our child(ren) surprise us, challenge us, and defy the expectations we constructed when we contemplated childbirth. Sometimes, our experience with parenting looks nothing like we had been taught to expect.

- What do you find most difficult about being a mother, and how do you handle it?

- Is 'normal' a realistic or even desirable goal for our children?

- How do the expectations and dreams for the children/family we expected to have impact the reality of our mothering? Discuss your experience juggling expectations and your child's reality.

- What do you dream for your child(ren)? How much of those dreams stem from your own dreams for the world?

- Are your hopes for your children shaped by your own successes and failures in life?

- How has parenting changed you? In what ways has it not changed you enough?

Through the Generations

The experience of becoming a mother not only changes our relationship with our own parents but it has us seeing our own mothers through very different eyes.

- What did you learn about being a mother from your own mother? How did that learning occur?

- What has changed in the way you view and understand your own parents?

Pain

Not all families start in a traditional or even joyful way. But even with difficult beginnings, rich, loving families can still blossom.

- Has there been anything particularly difficult in your parenting experience? How did you cope? Was there sufficient support or did you have concoct your own?

- If you have a non-traditional family, how has that impacted your parenting style and your ability to be the parent you think you should be?

- How have the challenges changed as your children grow?

www.ingramcontent.com/pod-product-compliance
Lightning Source LLC
Chambersburg PA
CBHW071215090426
42736CB00014B/2832